Schools Council
Research Studies

Defining
Public Examination
Standards

T. Christie
G. M. Forrest

Macmillan Education

First published 1981

Published by
MACMILLAN EDUCATION LTD
Houndmills Basingstoke Hampshire RG21 2XS
and London
Associated companies throughout the world

Printed in Hong Kong

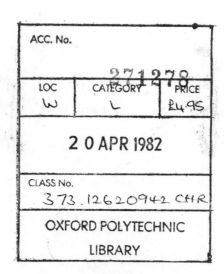
British Library Cataloguing in Publication Data

Christie, Thomas
Defining public examination standards. –
(Research studies/Schools Council)
1. General certificate of education
examination (Great Britain)
2. Grading and marking (Students) –
England
I. Title   II. Forrest, Gerald Moston
373.12′62   LB3056.G7

ISBN 0–333–31496–4

Contents

Tables and figures

Preface

The initial stimulus for this study was the authors' desire to comment at some length on the substantive implications of their pilot study of comparability of Advanced-level standards between 1963 and 1973. That study, however, was commissioned by the Schools Council as an investigation of the feasibility of a particular method and in the event it was decided that the report was not an appropriate vehicle for any exploration of the wide issues involved. (Christie and Forrest, 1980)

In the past five years our initial reactions to that study have been both clarified and modified by constant debate at the decision-making level on the appropriate interpretation and implementation of examination standards and inevitably many different people have contributed to our thinking during this period. Mr Christie expresses his gratitude to the Chairman, Pro-registrar and the Executive Subcommittee of the Schools Examinations Committee of the Caribbean Examination Council for their preparedness to consider the entire function of a public examination board *ab initio* and for the many lively debates which ensued. Mr Forrest has been deeply involved in such problems in relation to GCE examinations and in particular the technical problems of implementing the joint 16 + examinations for a wider ability range of pupils provided by the JMB and the consortia of CSE boards with which the JMB is associated.

For neither of us has GCE Advanced level been a primary focus of concern but we have retained that examination as our major examplar to avoid any necessity for lengthy description of new certificates and unfamiliar nomenclature. In our analysis of Advanced level we are deeply indebted to Mr C. Vickerman, Secretary-designate to the Joint Matriculation Board, for his critical comments on the entire text and for the enormous care he took to ensure that our interpretation of how JMB organizes its final meetings of examiners as they attempt to settle grade boundaries (see Chapter 4) does not depart too far from what happens in reality.

Nevertheless, it should be understood that the authors write in their personal capacities and that the ideas formulated here are their own responsibility. Although both are associated with the JMB (Mr Christie is one of the representatives of the University of Manchester on the Board and Mr Forrest is the Board's Director of Research), it must not be assumed that any of the views expressed are necessarily those of the JMB. They are views which have grown out of our professional involvement with examinations and represent our interpretation of the present position and of the future possibilities which might best serve the interests of our educational system.

June 1980

Abstract

This study seeks to explore the nature of the judgement that is required when examination boards are charged with the responsibility of maintaining standards. The argument is generalizable to any public examination structure designed to measure educational achievement, although in the interests of simplicity its exposition is confined largely to Advanced-level procedures, and in particular to those of the Joint Matriculation Board (JMB). Historical definitions of standards stress the importance of maintaining an equilibrium in examination practice between the definition of attainment by reference to a syllabus and by reference to the performance of other candidates. Present practice in the JMB is reviewed to see how this required equilibrium is maintained in the examiners' final meetings and, on the basis of an analysis of JMB statistics, it is concluded that the demands of comparability of standards between subjects and the demands of comparability of standards within a subject over time have diverged. A contest model of grading of the implementation of standards is adduced.

Two theoretical models of grading are then considered from the point of view of their goodness of fit to models of the nature of educational achievement. A third model—limen-reference assessment—is derived, which is thought to represent current practice in public examining boards: its properties and potential development are discussed. There appears to be no compelling theoretical reason for adopting any one of these models. Finally, the differing benefits of the approaches, emphasizing either parity between subjects or parity between years, are briefly reviewed in the context of four presumed functions of a public examination system, namely the provision of feedback to selectors, pupils, subject teachers and the wider society. In view of the imminent changes in certification at $16+$ and the continuing problems of sixth-form examinations it is hoped that this study will contribute to a debate culminating in an overt ordering of the priorities which should guide public examination boards in discharging their responsibility for maintaining standards.

'. . . the effect of competition is to keep up the standard' Macaulay
(*Hansard*, Vol. CXXVIII (3rd Series, col. 754: debate on the India Bill,
24 June 1853)

'But Shukhov—the guards could set the dogs on him for all he cared
now—ran back to have a last look. Not bad. He went up and looked over
the wall from left to right. His eye was true as a level. The wall was straight
as a die.'   Solzhenitsyn
(*One Day in the Life of Ivan Denisovich*, translated by Max Hayward and
Ronald Hingley)

The authors

The authors are G. M. Forrest, Director of Research at the Joint
Matriculation Board, and T. Christie, Senior Lecturer in Methods of
Educational Research at the University of Manchester.

1 Introduction

THE DUAL FUNCTIONS OF PUBLIC EXAMINATIONS

In the highly decentralized secondary education system of England, the role of the public examining bodies, themselves relatively autonomous, has been throughout the twentieth century as important as it is ill defined. Such is the influence of examinations on secondary education that shortly after its inception the Schools Council, charged with overseeing the curriculum and examinations for the 12–18 age group, could reiterate[1] in all seriousness that the curriculum must come first. That this rallying cry managed to avoid any hint of bathos is sufficient indication of the tensions in the secondary education system at that time, which had been there at least since the latter years of the Higher School Certificate.

> In practice, the First and Second School Examinations are in the nature of a compromise; in a greater or less degree several functions are combined in the Examinations . . . The Higher Certificate Examination is designed to test a certain part of the work of pupils at the advanced stage. But it has also to provide machinery for the award of State and, in some cases, University Scholarships and Local Education Authority awards. How far can it perform both functions satisfactorily? How far can the equilibrium of the examination be maintained? (Board of Education, 1939, pp. 19–21).

This overt recognition in 1938 of a potential tension between public examinations as summaries of current attainments and public examinations as prognoses of future performance was so disturbing that a special investigation was mounted into the workings of the Higher School Certificate in that year. Its report (Secondary School Examinations Council, 1939) covers criticisms made of the HSC which include, *inter alia*,

A   Failure to discharge with equal efficiency the two functions . . .
B   Lack of uniformity between one Examining Body and another in respect of:
   (i) The load of the examination.

1   One of the conclusions of the Spens Report was 'The School Certificate dominates the curriculum unduly. It should follow the curriculum, not determine it'. (p. 364. Board of Education, 1938).

(ii) The standard of difficulty of the papers.
(iii) The basis of recommendation of candidates for the award of Scholarships.
      (p. 8)

Forty years later the same issue of equilibrium emerged in a different guise. The Expenditure Committee of the House of Commons in its Tenth Report recommended

that examining boards strive to ensure that standards be kept as similar as possible:
  (i)   between the various boards
  (ii) between the various subjects
  (iii) from one year to the next
  (iv) between the various Mode II and Mode III schemes.
(House of Commons Expenditure Committee, 1977, para. 116).

The various elements of this equation have already been separately investigated. However, a brief review of the assumptions made in these various comparability studies will show that the definition of a proper equilibrium between the provision of a summary of current attainments and the provision of a prognosis of future performance is as much in need of investigation now as it was four decades ago.

ASSUMPTIONS UNDERLYING STUDIES OF COMPARABILITY OF STANDARDS

Between-board comparability

The necessity of maintaining comparability of standards between the various boards has been singled out for special emphasis in the Government Observations on the Tenth Report (1978, p. 4). A recent review of such comparability studies in the GCE sector (Bardell *et al.*, 1978) covers thirteen years of investigation and explores at length the conceptual and methodological problems involved.

Three major approaches to the investigation of inter-board comparability are identified. There is the straightforward comparison of the percentage passing in each board. Such a comparison assumes that the important criterion is opportunity and that each board should offer the same odds against successful completion of the examination. Offering shorter odds is unfair competition. But no simple comparison of the passing percentages in the various boards can establish whether the odds are longer or shorter since there are marked differences in each board's clientele. Thus, if it is a common standard of attainment that the boards must preserve, the surest prediction will be that passing percentages will differ from board to board. And indeed they do, though whether the degree of difference is systematically related to differences in their catchments has yet to be definitively established.

A second approach which figured largely in the Schools Council's monitoring of the establishment of CSE (Schools Council, 1966; Nuttall, 1971; Willmott, 1977) is to use a reference test. The grades of the various boards can then be compared by expressing the competence of the candidates in terms of the common scale provided by the reference test. The validity of such an approach depends on the extent to which the reference test enjoys an identical relationship with each of the examinations of the various boards. The test must not penalize any board by drawing on achievements not specified in its syllabus.

Bardell *et al.* (1978) deal in detail with two manifestations of such bias, the correlation between monitor and examination, and the mean score on the monitor. Obviously the highest correlations are to be anticipated from a monitor which is essentially a test of achievement based on the common core of all the syllabuses issued by all boards in any one subject.[1] But when there are real differences between examining boards in the achievements they label with a common subject name, the probability of establishing a subject achievement monitor capable of an unbiased estimate of between-board comparability is markedly reduced. And should the monitor exhibit only a low level of correlation with the various attainment tests to which it is referred doubts must arise about the interpretation of the findings since that correlation is the validity coefficient of the reference test.

With respect to the mean score the outcome is likely to be even less definitive:

... to a large extent the examination of the fairness of a monitor has to be subjective, since there is no way of distinguishing between biases in the monitor and the very differences in board standard which the exercise sets out to estimate. (Bardell *et al.*, 1978, p. 21).

Given those difficulties it has been found expedient—and cost effective— to retreat into a test which is uncontaminated by any of the achievements overtly specified in the subject syllabuses under scrutiny, but is nevertheless related to subject achievement. This approach, through a monitor designed to measure aptitude, has not been widely used in inter-board comparisons in the GCE sector but is the cornerstone of the early studies of the comparability of GCE and CSE grades conducted on behalf of the Schools Council. The assumption is that a candidate of given aptitude should have the same odds against achieving a given grade regardless of the board involved.

That assumption encapsulates the selection function of public examinations. It is quite at variance with the directive that the curriculum must come first in that it assumes that all syllabuses are uniformly effective

---

1   Newbould and Massey (1979) have produced an extended consideration of the problems associated with this approach.

in translating aptitude into achievement. The examining boards, especially in the GCE sector, have tried to avoid a complete commitment to that assumption by making a distinction between a teaching syllabus and an examination syllabus, but that distinction almost inevitably disappears in the statistical moderation of Mode III syllabuses.

What is a good syllabus? If the curriculum should come first, a good syllabus can be taken to be one which is so organized as to make the fundamental concepts and the *modus operandi* of the subject most readily accessible to the pupil. But, if the syllabus is claimed to be no more than an examination syllabus, it is primarily a delineation for the examiners of what is or is not 'fair game'. Nevertheless, even examination syllabuses can vary in the precision with which the relative importance of objectives and content is specified. The syllabus is a variable between aptitude and achievement and the comparability of grading cannot be established until the proper status of the syllabus is established.

To take an example, it is reported in the 1968 monitoring experiment (Nuttall, 1971, Table 7) that, in Chemistry, one CSE board differed from two others by about one grade on average. The implication is that a candidate of whatever aptitude would tend to receive a result from the first board which was one grade higher than the grade that would be awarded by either of the other two and that the discrepancy is in some sense an error. But does the analysis provide any evidence that the first board has assigned the wrong (too lenient) grade?

If the sole purpose of public examinations is selection, then the first board's grades are almost certainly wrong. Selectors tend to use GCE and CSE examination results as indicative of aptitude rather than as required achievements and there is no reason to suppose that the results of the common system of examining at 16 + will receive a different treatment.[1] They will still tend to ask for 'five Ordinary-level passes' rather than 'the successful completion of a five year secondary school course in Chemistry'. The notion of five unspecified passes depends upon a constant relationship being maintained, subject by subject, between aptitude and achievement, and the maintenance of such a relationship will require that the effectiveness of the syllabus is discounted.

---

1   In a Parliamentary answer to Mr Fred Silvester (Conservative, Manchester, Withington) on 19 February 1980 Mr Mark Carlisle, Secretary of State for Education and Science, outlined the Government's intentions with regard to the common system of examining at 16 + . 'In the light of our consultations the Government have decided in favour of reform based on two main principles:
   (i) the separate grading system of GCE O-level and CSE must be incorporated in a single consistent system of clearly defined grades;
   (ii) national criteria must be established for syllabuses and assessment procedures to ensure that all syllabuses with the same subject title have sufficient content in common, and that all boards apply the same performance standards to the award of grades.'

If one syllabus allows of more effective teaching than another it will lead to a higher level of achievement from students of comparable aptitude, but in so doing it will depart from the expected (i.e. average) relationships between achievement and aptitude and hence be identified on this analysis as a syllabus which has been too leniently graded. Conversely, should the other major function of the examination system, the certification of achievement, be held to be paramount there is no reason to suppose, on the evidence of an aptitude test as monitor, that one board is lenient in its grading practice in Chemistry. An equally valid response would be to scrutinize the syllabuses and the work of the subject panels in all three boards to establish by what means the first was able to so facilitate the teaching of Chemistry in its area that its candidates had been able to realize a markedly greater proportion of their potential than had the candidates in either of the other boards.

Such detailed scrutiny of actual achievement as revealed by the examination papers is the essence of the third kind of comparability study currently favoured by the GCE boards, the cross-moderation exercise (Bardell *et al.*, 1978). In such an exercise, scripts from one board are re-assessed by the nominees of other boards to see whether the same grades would have been awarded. The method enjoys the advantage that it depends upon human judgement which can allow for the differences in the objectives and priorities which are implicit in the mark schemes of different syllabuses having the same subject name. Such differences are the very *raison d'être* of the present practice in the GCE sector of allowing a choice of examining boards (and hence the continued existence of the boards themselves depends at least in part upon the assumption that the differences are non-negligible). The cross-moderation exercise, the technique which can take account of the differences, has recently become almost the standard approach to between-board moderation in the steady stream of investigations routinely mounted and financed by the CGE boards.

Unfortunately even chief examiners find difficulty in stating these differences explicitly and yet, until explicit criteria can be identified, the quantum of different syllabus demands cannot be measured. Hecker and Wood (1979) go so far as to conclude[1] on the basis of an investigation of Advanced-level Physics that when due attention is given in a cross-moderation study to agreeing the parameters by which the various examinations are to be evaluated, the study 'is bound to turn into an elucidation of the ways in which boards' examinations and outlooks differ' and that 'cut and dried verdicts concerning comparability of grading standards should not be expected' (Hecker and Wood, p. 20).

1   The authors were able to take into account the experience gained by Shoesmith and Massey (1977) in their study of Ordinary-level Mathematics.

To the sceptic this conclusion may smack of special pleading and not only on the grounds that the design of the particular investigation from which it stems was never fully implemented. The suspicion may be that negligible differences are being magnified in order to avoid drawing hard and fast and unwelcome conclusions about real differences in the standards demanded by the various GCE boards. After all, the Physics content of the four examinations under review was virtually indistinguishable in the multiple choice test and had at least 80 per cent in common in the written paper, and much the same situation obtains in History. Inglis (1980), on the basis of a content analysis of Ordinary- and Advanced-level History papers from two boards, could find no statistically significant differences either between boards or between examining levels in the weight given to different aspects of History.

However, to try to establish differences between boards on the basis of the content of their syllabuses is to adopt the wrong level of analysis; it is differences in the criteria by which marks are awarded which create problems for comparability of standards. The Ordinary-level English Literature study conducted by the Associated Examining Board (Houston, 1980) shares essentially the same paradigm as the Advanced-level Physics study and was carried through to the stage of a formal assessment of each sample of scripts. After much discussion the English Literature scrutineers (chief examiners from boards not included in the study) agreed three criteria, 'knowledge of set books', 'relevant use of knowledge' and 'expression of a personal response', and further that these should be equally weighted in arriving at overall judgements of the extent to which comparability of standards had been achieved by the four boards under scrutiny. They then evaluated samples of scripts from each board on each criterion and concluded that one board was out of line at one borderline. A further analysis of the data generated (Appendix A) reveals that, on the assumption of an equally weighted composite of the criteria, that conclusion is conservative indeed. But, more to the point, it is shown that no conclusions should be drawn on the basis of an equally weighted composite for the simple reason that each board differs in the emphasis it accords each criterion and for at least two of the boards the importance of a criterion varies according to which borderline is under review. Knowledge of set books, for instance, may be of paramount importance in removing a candidate from the ungraded category, but at the C/D boundary it may be subordinate to the use made of that knowledge in one board—but not in another where personal expression may now carry more weight. Only a comparison of composites reflecting these different emphases will produce a valid conclusion as to the comparability of the boards' standards.

The analysis in Appendix A is a statistical vindication of the GCE boards' assumption that there are real differences in the nature of the achievements they reward. Such differences by no means preclude the establishment of comparable standards—provided they can be identified in advance. In the English Literature study (Houston, 1980) the scrutineers, all of whom came from boards other than those under investigation, did not know what the differences in emphasis were until the end of the investigation—if then. A method of making such differences overt is described in Chapter 6. For the nonce let it be said that any approach to between-board comparability which does not honour the differences in the definition of subject achievement between boards is highly suspect.

The comparison of achievement at borderlines through cross-marking exercises is a potentially more valid approach to the study of inter-board comparability than is the comparison of passing percentages, or the derivation of expectations of passing from an external moderating test.

Criteria used in between-board comparability studies

While the methodologies of between-board comparability have been viewed as being quite distinct, the two criteria involved—aptitude and achievement—have been viewed almost as though they were inter-changeable, a mere matter of empirical expedience.

There has been some slight empirical justification for that view. 'On the only occasion that the results of a cross-marking experiment have been directly compared with the results of reference-testing, the agreement about standard was very good . . .' (Nuttall, 1971, p. 10). Unfortunately, one's view of 'very good' depends upon where one stands.

While no subsequent study comparing cross-moderation with the use of a reference test has come to hand, the opportunity arises in the report of the Advanced-level Physics Study (University of London Entrance and School Examinations Council, 1972) to compare the effects of an external aptitude test and an external achievement test as the monitor (Appendix B). The results are only indicative but point up a very real possibility of different conclusions being drawn about the comparability of a board's standards depending upon whether aptitude or subject achievement is the criterion of comparison even when the method of establishing compar-ability is held constant.

Further evidence for the empirical non-equivalence of the achievement and aptitude criteria is to be found in the Bloomfield *et al.* (1977) study of comparability between Mode I and Mode III examinations in Geography and Biology in two CSE boards. In each subject they used two external reference tests, Test 100, which measures aptitude, and a subject achieve-ment test. In Tables VI. 7 and VI. 14 of that report they give estimates of severity or leniency for each participating school made on the basis of each criterion separately. The correlation coefficient between the two estimates in thirty biology schools is $+0.73$ and in twenty-eight geography schools is

+0·82. These coefficients are high, as one might expect of predictions sharing a common feature. (Each pair of predictions consists of deviations from the same observed school mean grade.) Nevertheless, they indicate an overlap of no more than 50 to 60 per cent between the two bases of prediction. The practical consequences are there to be seen in the aforementioned tables. Bloomfield *et al.* suggest that adjustments would only be called for where severity or leniency estimates depart significantly from zero. Of the fifty-eight schools where comparison is possible the observed grades are 'correct' on either criterion in 30 instances. In a further eleven schools both criteria agree in indicating the school mean grade is 'wrong'. In the remaining seventeen schools whether the school mean grade is 'correct' or 'wrong' depends entirely upon whether aptitude or subject achievement is the criterion.

Conceptually, the two approaches are far from interchangeable. One takes aptitude as its measure and treats all differences in measured achievement as error; it is selection-orientated. The other takes achievement as its measure but is not well organized to give appropriate weight to circumstances in which that achievement is made manifest[1] so that the extent to which the examination achievement is representative of subject competence is difficult to evaluate. Nevertheless, it is closest in spirit to an attempt to render summaries of current attainments comparable.

Which of these criteria is the appropriate one for establishing comparability of standards between examining boards begs the question as to which of the dual functions of the examination system is to be paramount. Until that decision is made, the appropriateness of either approach to comparability of standards between boards must remain in doubt.

Between-subject comparability

Between-subject comparability has been investigated by Forrest (1971 *et seq.*) in GCE Ordinary level, by Nuttall *et al.* (1974) in GCE Ordinary level and CSE and by Kelly (1976) in the Scottish Higher Leaving Certificate. Nuttal *et al.* set out five major methods in this area of investigation, of which two are variants of the regression method described above. The other three[2] use an internally generated average achievement criterion rather than an externally measured aptitude criterion. Although they all appear very different they are all based on the same fundamental comparison. If, for all the candidates offering a given pair of subjects, the

1   Cross-moderation exercises are focused on examination papers and what is written in response to them. Thus they tend to overlook the adequacy of the sampling of the syllabus by the examination. Yet it is this latter feature as evidenced by the predictability of questions—the extent to which the examination can be 'spotted'—which for the candidate is a major index of examination difficulty. The aptitude approach takes account of the effect without being able to identify it.
2   One of these is the subject pairs technique used in Chapter 5.

mean grade for each of the two subjects is calculated, a comparison between the performances of the candidates in the two subjects is possible. If —while retaining a specified subject common to all pairs —the number of pairs is extended, it is possible to see how candidates offering that subject perform in the others and so measure the candidates' calibre in terms of their performance in the other subjects.

Clearly, comparison of the relative difficulty of subjects cannot proceed by comparison of achievements since these are necessarily subject specific. The internally generated average achievement criterion is therefore treated as an aptitude variable. Nuttall and his co-workers assume but one function for the public examination system, that 'examination results ought to reflect the general ability of candidates' (p. 5). So committed are they to this view that they base their adjustments against the external aptitude criterion on a 'mean pooled within-school regression coefficient of grade on test score' (p. 93), a statistic specifically designed to discount most of the effects of teaching on the relationship between aptitude and achievement. However, they do admit, that, if GCE and CSE examinations are graded as summaries of current attainments, comparability of standards between subjects is a 'red herring' (p. 68).

The internally generated average achievement criterion has been used by the main research workers in this field. They all proceed on the basis that 'if a large group of candidates representative of the population took, for example, both English and Mathematics, their average grades should . . . be the same'. (op. cit. p. 12). The fundamental assumption here is either that aptitude is unitary or that, if there are many specific aptitudes, these all occur with the same frequency in any cohort of candidates.[1]

Such assumptions are not lightly to be made. The very nature of ability or aptitude is an extremely contentious issue (touched on in Chapter 6 below) and thus its distribution is indeterminate.

Nevertheless, the tendency of different subjects—by their very nature to be more or less demanding of different aptitudes—is firmly to be resisted if comparability between subjects is to be maintained. Nuttall and Wilmott (1972) carry the argument to its logical conclusion.

Why have subject examinations at all? . . . For ranking purposes, then, if a single general intelligence test yields as much information as a series of subject examinations, why not give the teacher freedom to teach in his own way (i.e. along the lines of CSE Mode III) without the onus of an examination in each and every subject? A challenging thought! (p. 130).

It would be the more challenging were the problem of the nature of

1   This methodology involves parallel assumption to the regression method. Except in the special case where the candidates' choices of subjects can be deemed to be random, it is a requirement of all variants of the internally generated criterion approach that the correlation coefficients between every pair of subjects in the analysis are of similar size.

general intelligence closer to resolution. Two possible resolutions do in fact emerge from the between-subject comparability studies, the average examination grade and the total examination grade. But these indices of aptitude can only be won by completely subjugating the definition of attainments to the predictive function of public examinations.

Comparability between years

At first sight the techniques of between-subject comparability are applicable to the problem of maintaining comparability between years (see Kelly, 1976, Table 4). However, the technique is not addressed to the central issue in the maintenance of standards over time: does more really mean worse? If an increase in the size of the examination entry were to have this effect on —and to the same extent in —every examination subject, the relative status of the subjects would remain the same while the attainments defined by a grade in every subject drifted in unison.

Some discussion of the methodological problems associated with the investigation of the stability of standards over time will be found in Christie and Forrest (1980). They concluded that only a cross-moderation technique would resolve the issue. They introduced quasi-experimental controls in an attempt to quantify the effect of differences of emphasis in syllabus, in mark schemes and in the present standards of senior examining teams (the major areas of weakness in the cross-moderation approach).

Concern for the maintenance of standards over time is as one-sided as concern for between subject comparability: it speaks only to the function of describing attainments—the demands on aptitude to realize these attainments cannot be established from a scrutiny of candidates' performances in the examination room.

Between-mode comparability

Comparability of standards between modes has been studied by Nuttall (1973) in The West Yorkshire and Lindsey Regional Examining Board. The board has institutionalized a complex system of agreement trials (which belong to the family of cross-moderation exercises). Nuttall accordingly chose a methodology 'that is independent of and distinct from the normal moderation procedures of the Board' (p. 4), the regression of aptitudes as measured by Test 100 on grades awarded under Modes I, II and III. As might be expected, there is less than perfect concordance between the results based on the comparison of attainments and the results based on the comparison of aptitude and, as with interboard comparability studies, no means of resolving the discrepancies in the absence of a clear ordering of priorities in relation to the dual function of public examinations.

Between-mode comparability shares precisely the same problems as between-board comparability and within-subject comparability, but it is a consideration of the latter issue which best encapsulates the problem. It has been estimated that in the north of England there are over 10 000 separate examination syllabuses which will come under the umbrella of the proposed common system of examining at 16+ and certainly the examination of three quarters of a million candidates under Mode III arrangements in England and Wales in 1977 (Department of Education and Science, 1979) would tend to confirm that estimate[1]. Yet fewer than fifty identifiable subjects are involved in this plethora of syllabus provision.

Clearly, there will be a pressing need to establish the comparability of standards between syllabuses in the new 16+ examination system. Equally clearly, a directive to establish comparability of standards between boards, between subjects, within subjects and across time is too vague to shape such a system. Any structural reorganization of the public examination system at 16+ is going to have to take cognisance of the dual functions of that system. If the present multiplicity of definitions of attainment implicit in syllabuses is maintained, then paradoxically the very logistics of maintaining comparability enforce the use of a general ability test as monitor and the selection function—the certification of aptitude rather than achievement—will become paramount. If an attempt is made to identify, if not a core curriculum, then a core syllabus in each subject[2], cross-moderation becomes feasible and the definition of achievement takes precedence over the prediction of future success.

Thus there are organizational implications of the dual functions of public examinations. Immediately following the publication of the Waddell Report (Department of Education and Science, 1978) and the subsequent White Paper, attention focused almost exclusively on the organizational structures for the administration of the common system of examining at 16+. We cannot presume to comment on such matters. But by starting at the other end, with function rather than structure, and in particular with the problem of whether the duality of function can be maintained, we hope to provide a useful perspective on the kind of administrative structure which might best serve secondary school education.

We argue from past and present experience. For reasons of simplicity, most of the argument is confined to a consideration of GCE Advanced-level examinations, since these have been stable over a long period of time. However, Advanced level is only our chosen exemplar of the issue which arises at any level of public examining including 16+, that is, the issue of

1   Even on the generous assumption that the average school-based syllabus accommodates 150 candidates per annum, that figure would suggest 50 000 syllabuses at the 16+ level.
2   Present Government policy seems to be taking us in this direction: see footnote, p. 4.

the appropriate equilibrium among the various types of comparability. It is to the definition of an appropriate equilibrium between examinations as definitions of attainment and examinations as prognoses of future success, rather than to the success with which any one type of comparability is maintained, that the standards debate should be addressed.

2 The historical legacy

CONTINUITY IN STANDARDS

The GCE was introduced in 1951 when Advanced level replaced the Second Examination which was generally known as the Higher School Certificate. GCE Advanced level was from the start officially a pass/fail examination. From 1953, four categories of pass were recognized for purposes of communicating results to Local Education Authorities but only 'Distinction' or 'Pass' were recorded on certificates. Following the Third Report of the Secondary Schools Examination Council (1960) a seven-grade system of recording results (in terms of five passing grades and two failing grades) was introduced in 1963 and has remained in use ever since. The grading scheme is based on notional norms expressed in terms of proportions of candidates. As given in the Third Report these norms are as follows:

Grade	Percentage of entry	Cumulative percentage
A	10	10
B	15	25
C	10	35
D	15	50
E	20	70
O*	20	90
F	10	100

*Allowed Ordinary

Although it was emphasized in the Third Report that 'All the above percentages are to be regarded as no more than rough indications' (Secondary School Examinations Council, 1960, p. 27), stress was laid on the importance of ensuring that the proportion of candidates awarded grade C was not allowed to deviate markedly from the suggested norm.[1]

---

1 In 1969 the Schools Council expressed the hope that the boards would not adhere rigidly to the suggested distribution of grades regardless of the calibre of the candidates (letter to the boards of 27 February 1969 from Mr. W. G. Easeman, a Chief Executive Officer at the Schools Council). Inspection of the boards' published statistics enables one to see how closely the 'norms' are now followed: that some boards in some subjects include many more than 10 per cent of the candidates in grade C is apparent.

In framing this grading scheme it was assumed that the 'standard of pass would remain unaltered' (Secondary School Examinations Council, 1960, p. 8), an explicit directive that comparability of standards over time should be maintained. The standard amounted to the expectation, then current, of a 70 per cent pass which had been taken directly from the percentage of candidates attaining a Higher School Certificate (Table 1). The most recently published national statistics for Advanced level show that when GCE grade awards are aggregated over all subjects and all boards in England and Wales they conform closely to the SSEC passing norm which was confirmed in 1960 (last two rows of Table 2). Little variation is to be found from year to year in this aggregate at the pass or any other grade level. But in recent years sixth-formers have increased substantially in numbers, in academic range, and in the variety of their aspirations (Schools Council and Standing Conference on University Entrance, 1973).

It may be that the influence of these changes on Advanced-level attainments has been cancelled out by a concomitant increase in the variety of subjects offered at Advanced level, by a move away from a sole reliance on essay format in examining, or by a change of approach by sixth form teachers. It may be that the changes simply have not affected Advanced-level attainments. Or it may be that the overall stability in passing percentage is entirely a function of examination procedure. It will be seen from Tables 1 and 2 that the HSC actually provided two guidelines. Table 1 reports that just under 70 per cent of candidates were awarded the group HSC certificate whereas Table 2 indicates that the pass rate aggregated over the principal individual subjects of the HSC was just below 75 per cent. The latter index is the closer analogy to the GCE situation but the transition

Table 1   Numbers of candidates entered and passed in the Approved Second Examination (Higher School Certificate)

Year	Number of pupils entered	Number of pupils passed	Pass per cent
1938*	13 202	9 514	72·1
1947†	26 322	18 701	71·0
1948*	29 731	20 582	69·2
1949*	32 656	22 093	67·7
1950*	34 364	23 447	68·2

(Data for the years 1939–1946 are not available)

* Ministry of Education, 1951, Table 30
† Ministry of Education, 1948(a), Table 32

Table 2   Numbers of subject entries and percentages attaining the pass level in HSC and GCE Advanced level

Year	Examination	Number of subject entries	Number of 'passes'	Pass per cent
1938*	Second (HSC principal subjects)	36 951	29 039	78·6
1947†	Second (HSC principal subjects)	78 069	59 313	76·0
1948*	Second (HSC principal subjects)	88 518	66 114	74·7
1949*	Second (HSC principal subjects)	96 767	71 112	74·5
1950*	Second (HSC principal subjects)	101 903	75 464	74·1
1951‡	GCE Advanced level	103 800	76 300	73·5
1959‡	GCE Advanced level	184 600	126 700	68·6
1976§	GCE Advanced level	533 296	362 852	68·0

* Ministry of Education, 1951, Table 30
† Ministry of Education, 1948(a), Table 32
‡ Ministry of Education, 1960, Appendix B
§ Department of Education and Science, 1978(b), Table 27

was made in the atmosphere of the following directive, albeit regarding standards at Ordinary level, in a letter from the Ministry of Education to the examining boards (Ministry of Education, 1948 (b)).

As the Minister made clear in the Circular[1], his chief desire is that standards should not merely be maintained but, so far as possible, raised and he wants to see a high standard set from the outset and kept up in the interests of all concerned. He considers that the entry of unsuitable candidates, which may in the early years result from parental pressure on the schools, should be discouraged, if necessary by failures on a large scale; if it continued, with or without a further and lower pass standard, it would tend to affect syllabuses and types of paper and would defeat the object which he has in mind.
The Minister recognises that there will be a transitional problem in 1951 just for one year. At first sight it might appear that the somewhat less exacting standard for a pass at the ordinary level in 1951, described in paragraph 14(b), will make it difficult for those Universities which wish to satisfy themselves about a pupil's general level of attainment.

There is a clear implication that the more severe standard was carried as a matter of policy and that the stability of passing percentages over several decades is a feature of the interpretation of the standard to be maintained rather than a reflection of the actual standards of attainment in the schools.

It is rather unlikely then that the SSEC standard has been interpreted as the standard of attainment which was met by about 70 per cent of the 1950

1   Ministry of Education Circular 168 (23rd April 1948) announced the introduction of the GCE examination for 1951.

and earlier cohorts, but it is a distinct possibility that it has been interpreted as the statistical expectation which any candidate in any year should have of obtaining a subject pass. Most probably the reality is some ill-defined compromise between the two.

THE AVAILABLE DEFINITION OF THE
ADVANCED-LEVEL STANDARD

This potential ambiguity in interpretation has its origins in the transition from the Higher School Certificate to the GCE system. In proposing the GCE system the Secondary School Examinations Council (1947) had this and only this to say on the topic of GCE Advanced-level standards:

21(c) The 'Advanced' papers shall be designed to provide a reasonable test in the subject for pupils who have taken it as a specialist subject for two years of 'Sixth Form' study . . .

Standards:
27. We are anxious that any effect which the examinations may have on standards of work should be beneficial and stimulating . . .
29. We recommend that a 'Pass' at 'Advanced' level should approximate closely to what has been the 'Pass' standard in the Higher School Certificate examination.

To modern eyes these statements appear anodyne, but the report and more particularly the effects of the report on the fifth year candidates caused a furore ' . . . the wrath of the schools descended upon the examining bodies with loud lamentations about "slaughter of the innocents"' (Petch, 1953, p. 175). Petch attributes the lamentations to a failure to appreciate that an Ordinary-level pass was to be equated to a School Certificate credit. More to the point, he goes on:

Other features of the scheme emphasize its severity. The School Certificate and the Higher School Certificate were both awarded on overall performance; good work could on occasion and within limits compensate for weakness. (op. cit., p. 175)

For example, in 1947 and again in 1948, about 500 candidates (approximately 7 per cent of the successful candidates) in the JMB HSC examination were awarded a certificate as a result of 'compensation' in one subject.

The transition from HSC to GCE was a transition from a group certificate to a single-subject examination. A group certificate is focused on the candidate. The compensation procedure at the HSC borderline made this quite clear: the candidate's pattern of strengths and weaknesses was under review with little if any reference back to the actual scripts he had written. In contrast the focus of an Advanced-level borderline review, as conducted in the JMB and other boards, is on a review of those elements of the scripts which appear most likely to reveal evidence of subject mastery. It is subject attainment that is certified and it is within that very different context that the SSEC guidelines are now to be interpreted. Yet at the same time as it instigated a quite different philosophy of certification the SSEC remained silent on how the standard should be carried across that divide.

THE OPERATIONAL DEFINITION OF THE HIGHER SCHOOL CERTIFICATE STANDARD

The silence is instructive. Significantly, Petch (1953) too, in the twenty pages he devotes to 'Transition to the General Certificate of Education 1951', makes no mention of a problem in this regard. The potential problem had disappeared with the operationalization of the Higher School Certificate standard.

In 1914, Circular 849 (*Examinations in Secondary Schools. Proposals of the Board of Education*) defined the standard for the group School Certificate in terms of individual subjects thus:

The standard for a *pass* will be such as may be expected of pupils of reasonable industry and ordinary intelligence in an efficient secondary school. The form and not the pupil will be the unit for examination, and it is contemplated that a large proportion of the pupils in the form should be able to satisfy the test.

Petch comments on 'the impossibility of reaching a work-a-day solution in such terms as those' (op. cit., p. 99). He adopts a quite unambiguous position which he claims had been JMB policy since 1921. The Board based its subject standardization on the assumption that

in any one year the work of 20,000 candidates from hundreds of schools will be much the same in quality as was the work of the twenty thousand candidates drawn in similar conditions from the same field who offered the same subject in the previous year, and in the years before that . . . That the candidates themselves are to set the standard has always been a hard saying for those who hold that the examiner knows . . . Leaving aside such matters as temperament, health and tedium, no examiner can have a stable idea of an absolute standard applicable in all cases and in all circumstances. And what holds for one examiner also holds for a group of examiners working as a panel. (op. cit., pp. 143–145)

The initial impetus towards public examinations for school leavers lay in the rationing of scarce resources. Results were used almost exclusively for university selection or entry to a single profession (Secondary School Examinations Council, 1960) and hence the demand was for a ranking on some single scale which looked as though it might be predictive of later success. The basic difficulty in arriving at such a ranking from performance in different subjects or groups of subjects had been known since the inception of the mental testing movement: the 'lack of commensurate units in measuring the phenomena of education' (Thorndike, 1905, p. 444) or, as Aristotle has it, 'all men do not honour the same virtue'. Chief examiners

include historians, scientists, linguists, each with his own view of rewardable behaviour. But each is required to answer the selector's question:
'Is Jean better at English than John is at Mathematics?'. The response to
that conundrum was provided by J. M. Crofts (Secretary to the Joint
Matriculation Board, 1919 – 1941), who is credited with the idea of using
the cumulative percentile curve—'ingenious and bold' in the view of the
HSC Investigators (Secondary School Examinations Council, 1927)—
ingenious, bold and uncompromising. Crofts and Jones (1928) describe
how the work of assistant examiners is standardized and continue:

. . . we have, in fact, imposed the standard of the chief examiners on the whole
panel, but what guarantee have we that this standard is the correct one? What units
have the chief examiners to measure by? Actually none whatever. (p. 44)

The solution was to reject any subject specific criterion.

If the marks obtained by all the candidates in a subject are placed in order of merit,
we can then see how many candidates obtain each mark in the scale; we can find
how many obtain 100 per cent, how many obtain 99 per cent, and so on down to 0
per cent. If, then, we plot percentage of marks against percentage of candidates, we
get what is called a curve of distribution (p. 5). If this is done for all subjects, it is
found that, though a variety of shapes is obtained, the curves for subjects of an
elementary standard fall into two groups (see Fig. 3), in one of which are found
Foreign Languages, Mathematics, and Sciences, and in the other, English, History,
Geography, Scripture, Art, etc. The curves in the first group are much flatter than
those in the second group; that is to say, few candidates score very low marks and
few score very high marks in English subjects as compared with Mathematics and
Science, etc. Such differences in curves are persistent: they occur year after year. We
always get the two types with the same general characteristics. The cause of the
difference is quite simple. It is possible for a candidate to get full marks for every
question in Mathematics; all he has to do is get the right answer in the right way. But
in English or History, what is the right answer? How often is a teacher or examiner
going to give 10 marks out of 10 for an answer in History? He will always say to
himself, "Well, I think so and so ought to have been mentioned." Similarly, for the
poor answer. In Mathematics nought is a frequently occurring mark, but in Group 1.
(English) subjects it is difficult for a teacher or examiner not to find some merit and
to award one or two marks.
    It is a fact, then, from differences inherent in the subjects themselves, that in any
normal distribution of marks the percentage of candidates obtaining 75 per cent of
the maximum marks in English is less than the percentage obtaining that same mark
in Mathematics. (pp. 49–50)
    In a large examination is there any reason for thinking that the candidate who is
this 90th percentile in Mathematics has a better brain, is a more capable scholar, is a
better subject for the award of a scholarship than the candidate who occupies that
position in English, or, for the matter of that, in any other subject? There is no
evidence whatever in favour of this; the case cannot be proved one way or the other,
and it would be unwarrantable to assume that any difference does exist. (pp. 69–70)

By locating the English performance relative to the performance of all English candidates and the mathematics performance relative to the performance of all mathematics candidates an answer to the selection problem is arrived at. A distinction performance refers to the work of the best candidates available—the general prediction which was substituted for a plethora of specific predictions by the introduction of the Higher School Certificate and subsequently extrapolated uncritically into GCE. A commensurate unit in education has been assumed: man is, indeed, the measure of all things.

To take the candidate as unit of measurement as the 'curve' does will allow of equating standards between subjects, if certain assumptions are made. The concept of ability is central to many attempts to standardize. To fix the grades in any subject by reference to the performance of the candidates in all other subjects they attempt, as is basic to the Australian system, is to accept a single general academic ability—hence 'academic' standards. To scale internal school awards on a small battery of external tests as happens in Sweden (Marklund, 1969) is to accept a small number of abilities—hence standards of literacy and numeracy. To assume that the same distribution of award should be made in every subject, Croft's ingenious and bold solution is to leave the ability assumption open without necessarily avoiding it. One can take it that a general ability equally implicated in all subjects is implied or that each subject draws upon its own specific ability, such abilities being similarly distributed in each cohort of subject candidates or that what is implied is a relatively few general abilities with each subject drawing upon a commensurate subset. Any of these ability assumptions can be taken to underly the five-Ordinary-levels standard or the two-Advanced-levels standard.

Furthermore it is not an escape to assume that it is achievement which is standardized, not ability, since application of the cumulative percentile curve then involves further assumptions covering all the determinants of academic achievement: *inter alia*, that opportunities for learning are the same in all subjects, that the quality of instruction does not differ, that all subjects are equally interesting, that the extrinsic motivation arising from their buying power in the market place is identical, and so on. In short, to accept the 'curve', an early and particularly pure exemplar of what is nowadays referred to as norm-referenced measurement, as the appropriate method for ensuring between-subject comparability is simultaneously to idealize the attainment construct and to deny the very notion of an absolute achievement standard which has to be carried. And once standards are no longer absolute the transition from a group to an individual subject certificate is no longer a difficulty.

Petch himself is fully aware that the norm-referenced system he advocates can only ensure continuity under certain circumstances of which one is that 'there must be no reason to think that the nature of the entry has been subjected to arbitrary change' (op. cit., p. 146). What could be more arbitrary than a complete reorientation of the frame of reference of the grading system? A sole reliance on the standardization procedure which was in operation in JMB in 1953 implies that, no matter what the SSEC or the Expenditure Committee of the House of Commons should require, continuity of standards of attainment simply cannot be guaranteed. To change the framework of the assessment is to invite the choice, equally arbitrary, of a new percentage of passes.

3 Competing perspectives on the standards problem

GENERALITY OF THE NORM-REFERENCED SOLUTION

The United States, Sweden and—as we have seen—Britain, three countries with very different administrative structures for educational assessment, all rely to some extent on a norm-referenced approach. In pure norm-referenced measurement the quality attributed to an individual's performance is based on his position relative to the other examinees, that is, his place in a rank order. The meaningfulness of the individual score emerges from its relation to the scores attained by other examinees, the norm group.

Public examination systems usually have sufficiently large entries to claim that their norm groups are representative of specified sections of national populations. Sweden, with a single national examination board, need not specify the population of examinees too closely: questions of inter-board comparability do not arise. Nevertheless the norm-referenced approach still poses problems for the Swedes. Husén (1974, pp. 30–1) reports:

The 1940 Royal Commission on schools made a thorough inquiry into the route travelled by pupils through the lower secondary academic school (*real skola*). By and large, it was found that two out of every three starters reached the point of qualifying for admission to the *gymnasium* or pre-university school. One out of every two completed the course without having to repeat a grade. These findings pertained to conditions in the late 1930's and early 1940's when roughly one sixth of every [age] cohort went to lower secondary school or its equivalent. Analogous inquiries were made by the 1957 Governmental School Commission . . . 'notwithstanding the fact that admissions. . . to lower secondary academic school [had more than doubled] it was found that the percentages of non promotions and drop outs held at the same levels.'

The phenomenon is a familiar and equally contentious one in Britain. In the United States the comparability problems raised by the norm-referenced approach are worse compounded. Private corporations are responsible for the production of most assessment material but have consistently failed to agree on even a common frame of reference with which to describe their norm groups (Lennon, 1972).

That dimension of the problem also has its English counterpart. Different GCE boards and, even more so, different subjects are known to attract different clienteles. Unfortunately there is little consensus and even less systematic research on the crucial differentiating characteristics of populations with regard to public examination achievement. Bardell *et al.* (1978) draw attention to the readily overlooked influence of the proportion of girls in the norm group. Girls, if candidates, tend to be better achievers than boys, and the situation is worse compounded by an interaction with the subject of study. Nuttall *et al.* (1974), in relation to GCE/CSE, and Kelly (1976), in relation to the Scottish Certificate of Education, independently report the same pattern. The physical sciences (Chemistry, Physics and Mathematics) yield lower grades to girls than to boys; languages (German, French and English) yield lower grades to boys than to girls. In the Kelly study these differences were consistent over four successive years.

The impact of the social class composition of the norm group is less clear cut. Kelly's analysis did not produce any evidence of a distortion from this source in between-subject comparability, although both Miles (1973) in England and Weir (1975) in Scotland found the same extreme trend:

. . . an undue proportion of able children from lower socio-economic groupings do not choose subjects high in the [sic] academic esteem and similarly an undue proportion of less able children from the higher socio-economic grouping do not choose subjects low in the academic hierarchy' (Weir, 1975, p. 7).

The effect is perhaps confounded with the rather more obvious but not necessarily more important impact of type of centre. Musgrove (1971), for example, draws a distinction between the 'over-potent' and the 'merely potent' school, the former occurring with greater than chance frequency among independent, direct grant and grammar schools. While admitting that their characteristics are not well defined he equates over-potent schools with highly structured environments which, while designed specifically to enhance the probability of gaining Advanced-level qualifications, rob these same qualifications of any predictive efficiency for future success.[1] Advanced-level qualifications gained in a less 'pressurized' environment, he opines, may signal 'more intellectually autonomous people.' (p. 18)

It is the recurrent theme of the pre-war reports, qualification versus prognostication, brought up to date. The equilibrium between the two is now seen to be displaced first one way, then another, according to the pre-examination experience of the candidates. The Wankowski study, on which

1   Wankowski (1969) found that Advanced-level results from independent, direct grant and grammar schools are relatively poor predictors of university success; they predict well in the case of students from relatively unselective and comprehensive schools.

Musgrove's analysis is based, merits replication in view of its important implications for the interpretation of GCE Advanced-level results. It suggests the need for a systematic effort to establish whether the attainments of pupils should or can be examined without giving undue weight to the contribution of their teachers and some public debate on how 'undue' might be defined. It is the failure of studies of inter-board and inter-subject comparability to identify problems at this level of analysis which accounts for their less than cumulative impact.

What can be concluded from the studies conducted so far is that subject comparability within a board is held within a fairly close conformity to explicit assumptions (Forrest and Smith, 1972; Nuttal *et al.*, 1974; Welsh Joint Education Committee, 1973). But, notwithstanding the generally optimistic conclusions of within-board comparability studies, there is no doubt that comparability of standards has not always been achieved among boards either in HSC (Secondary School Examinations Council, 1939) or in GCE (University of London School Examinations Council, 1972; Scott, 1975; Shoesmith *et al.*, 1977). Such unpredictability in the criterion is itself a block to systematic studies of the appropriate defining characteristics of the norm group, those which most directly influence achievement.

The problems arising from fluctuations in the norm group are not confined to GCE. The terms of reference of CSE boards defined one reference point for standards as follows: 'a 16 year-old pupil of average ability who has applied himself to a course of study regarded by teachers of the subject as appropriate to his age, ability and aptitude, may reasonably expect to secure grade 4' (Secondary School Examinations Council, 1963, p. 122). At the outset it was envisaged that the 'CSE system of subject examinations should be designed for a band of candidates extending from those taking the ordinary level of the GCE examination, to those who are just below the average in ability'. But a Schools Council survey (1975 (a)) revealed that in every subject area candidates are drawn from a greater range of ability than anticipated in the original design of both the GCE and the CSE examinations. Fifty-two per cent of the age group were taking at least one O-level and 68 per cent at least one CSE with over 90 per cent at 'a conservative estimate' (p. 36) entered for at least one public examination in summer 1974.

Such figures are not in themselves inconsistent with the idea that the two examination systems are catering only for the upper 60 % of the ability range in any given subject. Incontrovertible evidence to the contrary arises, however, from the figures for English and Mathematics (op. cit., p. 36).

It further appears that the range of candidate ability is wider than expected in Art, Biology, Geography, History and Religious Education, 'while for

French, Physics and Chemistry, candidates are selected almost exclusively from the top half of the ability range' (op. cit., p. 37).

Weir (1975) reports a similar extension of the ability cohort *vis-à-vis* the Scottish Certificate of Education, especially among the higher socio-economic groups. What is the implication of these figures? Has the meaning of CSE Grade 4 changed or was it never in accord with its official definition? Public examination boards just do not know enough about the characteristics of the subject entries to answer such a question. They are aware of the attainments of candidates but not of how these attainments are brought about.

Changes over time in the raw mark distributions upon which grade decisions are based can be due either to the characteristics of the particular questions set, or to the marking scheme, or to the characteristics of the particular individuals who make up the entry—or to some combination of these factors. In Sweden and the USA, Scotland and Australia, and, in the final analysis, in England few systematic attempts are made to disentangle them. The raw mark distribution, which is likely to be a close reflection of actual achievement, is not reported and the grades are a straightforward numerical translation of the rank order. All five countries have ducked a not intractable problem, losing baby and bathwater in the process. The requirement of following, even in general terms, the grade norms of established custom, has brought the achievement of comparability of opportunity between subjects into conflict with the need to stress year-to-year comparability of attainment.

Given the evidence of Tables 1 and 2 (p. 17) and the international acceptance of the norm-referenced solution to the grading problem, it is tempting to conclude that the GCE boards chose to carry forward not the Higher School Certificate standard of achievement, even as operationally defined in terms of a percentage of the cohort, but simply the 70 per cent expectation of reaching that standard. Certainly the remarkable stability from one year to the next in grade percentages of large entry subjects must reinforce the belief of those who assert that GCE boards pass a given percentage of subject entries each year. Such a strategy, if adopted, does not guarantee comparability of attainment over time. It may not even represent comparability of opportunity over time. But as long as selection, in particular university selection, is the major function of the GCE system such comparability really does not matter. On the other hand it is now the case that only about one third of advanced-level candidates aspire to university education. Not only the circumstances of the candidates but also the potential functions of sixth-form examinations are undergoing change. It is an open question whether present examination practices have taken any account of these developments.

RESUSCITATION OF THE JUDGEMENT OF EXAMINERS[1]

Sentiments such as those expressed by Petch (quoted on p. 17 above) in defence of subject standardization are hardly designed to recommend themselves to the persons of undoubted subject matter expertise who act as chief examiners for the boards. It was the paramount importance of State Scholarship awards in the inter-war years which led at an early stage to the subordination of the judgement of chief examiners (in the JMB at least) to the exigencies of between-subject comparability.

. . . in November 1921, the difficulties involved in considering Scholarship awards to candidates who offered different subjects were becoming acute and the HSC examiners, *some of whom were proving a little obdurate over what they regarded as an infringement of their prerogative*, were instructed that it was essential 'to equate the examination values of the different subjects'. On October 18, 1923, the Board first, officially, heard from Crofts of 'the curve' . . . .

'(Petch, 1953, p. 138—italics added)'

Paradoxically, it was the transition to the single subject GCE system, a system which exacerbates the between-subject comparability problem that 'the curve' was designed to solve, which led to a rehabilitation of the judgement of examiners, albeit in more covert form.

The 70 per cent norm is only applicable to individual subjects on the assumption that each subject attracts a representative sample from the entire Advanced-level cohort with respect to the expectation that a pass would have been attained in the Higher School Certificate. That assumption appears to have been rejected both by the boards and by the SSEC at an early stage. Even though inter-board differences are by no means negligible, there are individual subjects and groups of allied subjects which depart consistently from the SSEC norm. Between 1970 and 1976, for example, the percentage of candidates in Latin in England and Wales awarded a grade E or better increased from 80·7 to 86·3 while the number of candidates dropped from 5120 to 2883; on the other hand, the domestic science subjects show lower percentages, particularly in the upper grades, than the expectations set out in the norms. The occasional appearance of a trend of this type will no doubt reassure those who, like Macintosh (1969), believe that the boards have a predetermined 'pass mark', an achievement standard.

1 'Let us first dispose once and for all of this high sounding title, examiner. The typical assistant examiner examines nothing: he marks scripts under the direction of Chief Examiners who prepare the papers and mark schemes. If it is a poor paper and poor mark scheme there is little that the marker of scripts can do about it. Experience as an assistant marker for a G.C.E. 'O' level examination, the Royal Society of Arts, and so on, gives one little claim to the title of examiner. There is no trained cadre of examiners in the true sense outside the ranks of a select band of Chief Examiners relying more on intuition and instinct than on job card analysis (Secondary School Examinations Council, 1964), item analysis, validation and the other factors identified in Examinations Bulletin No. 1.' (Secondary School Examinations Council, 1963). (Mather *et al.*, 1965, p. 65)

However, these departures[1] from the SSEC norms tend to be confined to subjects with relatively small entries and that was not the respect in which the judgement of examiners came into its own. The rehabilitation was much more pervasive. Nowhere in any of the published deliberations on the GCE system is the quantum of an Ordinary level or Advanced level explicitly defined. Yet, wherever there is a choice of subjects, justice requires that the various subjects be rendered equivalent. GCE with its single subject certification faces this problem of subject equivalence in an extreme form (as indeed does CSE). Little wonder then that a major effort of the GCE boards is directed towards the creation and maintenance of subjects which make essentially equivalent demands of candidates.

Unfortunately the very identity of subjects renders them somewhat intractable in this respect. Boards can in theory capitalize on the natural trade-off between breadth and depth in a timetable of fixed duration and make further adjustments in the examination itself by manipulating the extensiveness and predictability of syllabus sampling and the level at which questions are pitched. But these are all matters for expert judgement. Furthermore, the difficult task of ensuring comparability between subjects does not end there when there are no longer required groups of subjects. Subjects must be not only equivalent in demand but so defined that no undue easing of demand can be engineered by the choice of a particular combination of subjects. If an unavoidable advantage would accrue to a candidate through a particular combination it must be either proscribed in the board's regulations or downgraded in value. That there are only a moderate number of such proscriptions can be taken as a testament to the judgemental skills of the subject committees of the boards, for there is no sensible norm-referenced approach to syllabus construction.

The decision to incorporate new subject matter in a syllabus and its related examination inevitably is taken without knowledge of its effects on the mark distribution. Moreover, once a new element is included in an examination syllabus the idea can be disseminated with remarkable agility. Plate tectonics, for example, was undergraduate Geology in the 1950's but by the sixties had been incorporated in Advanced level and has now made a successful appearance in some Ordinary-level syllabuses. On the other hand, innovations occasionally misfire, or fail to take hold: the orbital theory of bonding as an Advanced-level Chemistry syllabus requirement is one such example. Nevertheless, even though new subject matter will often

1   Shoesmith et al., (1977) note that in relation to French at Advanced level, a large entry subject: 'The extent to which a board allows its grading to move away from the SSEC proportions in a given subject must in the end be a matter of judgement. There is evidence . . . that adjustments are made, in the appropriate direction, but they are probably not large enough to bring all standards for all boards into line. Indeed, if they were large enough , they might in some cases lead to grade distributions so different from the SSEC recommendations as to be unlikely to command popular credibility.' (p. 27)

have been tried out by teacher members of a syllabus development group before incorporation in the syllabus the recognition that 'in some respects, examinations have stimulated and facilitated curriculum change' (Schools Council, 1975 (b), p. 102) is essentially an acknowledgement of the value of giving free rein to the expert judgement of syllabus groups and their associated chief examiners. Had the facility values[1] of questions based on new syllabus material been invoked at an early stage it is likely that the wider dissemination of that material would have faltered. For a too heavy reliance on such normative information yields an immutability to the *status quo* which is quite unmerited and must inevitably tend towards the complete ossification of subjects. Change, flexibility and development in syllabuses can only come about as a result of decisions based on judgements of an absolute kind about what is and what is not appropriate to a particular subject at a particular level of education.

The capacity of expert subject teachers to make such judgements, long enshrined in the syllabuses of public examinations in Britain, has only recently been discovered in the United States, where it is now the cornerstone assumption of the criterion-referenced testing movement (Millman, 1973). Hambleton *et al.* (1978, p. 2) point out that 'criterion-referenced' is something of a misnomer:

For many individuals it refers to a performance standard, a minimum proficiency level, or a cut-off score. But it is clear from the two most influential criterion-referenced testing papers in the 1960's (Glaser, 1963, Popham and Husek, 1969) that these writers used the word 'criterion' to refer to a *domain* of behaviours.

Certainly our public examination question papers meet Popham's (1975) definition: 'A criterion-referenced test is used to ascertain an individual's status (referred to as a domain score) with respect to a well defined behaviour domain' (p. 130).

The recommended, indeed one might almost say the conventional, method of describing a domain for the purposes of sampling examination questions from that domain is the 'specification grid' (Bloom *et al.*, 1971). Such grids, while they vary in detail from subject to subject are conventionally presented as a rectangle with a levels-of-thinking axis and a content axis. The cells of the resulting matrix contain weights which are to be observed by the test constructor. GCE syllabuses tend to fall a long way short of such formalism, though in the JMB at least it is now the practice at

---

The selection of questions on the basis of their facility values, the proportions of a representative sample of the target population who respond correctly in a pre-test, is one hallmark of norm-referenced examination construction. The very nomenclature betrays the origins of norm-referenced assessment in attempts to identify stable individual differences (i.e. abilities or aptitudes). In the context of educational attainment, the more 'pre' the test, the less representative is the sample of the population for whom the test is intended.

each syllabus revision to include an overall weighting for generalized abilities to be tested. Nevertheless, some observers may object that the public examination system comes closer to Popham's (1974) 'cloud-referenced assessment' than to 'domain-referenced assessment' in that most examination syllabuses are straightforward statements of content with no levels-of-thinking axis to complete the traditional specification grid. However, the omission of a mental operations axis is not a serious one. Firstly, Bloom's categories refer to mental processes, not to observable events and it is notoriously difficult to establish just what operations any candidate used in framing his response to a question: this stricture applies just as cogently to essay questions as to multiple choice items. Secondly, 'despite recent advances in clarifying educational objectives, there can still be considerable variance in the intended or implicit level of sophistication with which a concept is developed, given ostensibly the same goals' (Anderson, 1969, p. 8).

Public examination syllabuses are intended to communicate intentions to teachers and in this respect the record of behavioural objectives, or more precisely of Bloom's (1956) taxonomy of such objectives, is hardly edifying. Fairbrother (1975) had twenty-two Physics teachers allocate forty Physics multiple choice items to levels of Bloom's taxonomy. In one experiment not a single item elicited perfect agreement among the raters. In a second experiment there was perfect agreement on only 7 per cent of the items. Seddon (1978), in a critical review of the utility of Bloom's taxonomy as a medium of communication concludes, 'It is likely that Fairbrother's results . . . are the most generalizable to real life educational contexts.' (p. 306). While it is possible that some of the successors of behavioural objectives reviewed by Hambleton *et al.*, (1978) such as 'amplified objectives' or 'item forms analysis' may make some contribution, it remains the case that in many content areas we are unlikely to be able to produce the clarity of domain specifications which some commentators, such as Ebel (1962) or Anderson (1969), feel is necessary if standards are to be expressed in terms of mastery of a domain. Anderson (op. cit.) points out that there are reasons to be cautious about a sole reliance on such standards; the notion of a percentage mark criterion, '90 per cent of what someone chose to teach and measure' (p. 8), he dismisses out of hand. But that is something of a straw man in the British context where Advanced-level syllabuses must be approved by the Schools Council. When similar anxieties are expressed in Britain it is almost entirely in relation to Mode III, whether in CSE, GCE or in the 16 + feasibility and development studies. Almost all Mode I syllabuses and their associated examinations have undergone a long and careful process of consensual validation: they do not refer to what any one person chose to teach and measure.

To this extent public examinations in England and Wales are already domain referenced. Only their definition of standards by reference to percentages of candidates distinguishes GCE examinations from criterion-referenced assessments. And that distinction may no longer be as clear cut as Petch (1953) once described. Had Bayesian theory (cf. Novick and Jackson, 1974) been available to them with the necessary computational facilities, HSC review panels might well have welcomed a peculiarly powerful formalization of their own less structured deliberations in the borderline review procedure. Bayesian estimates can reduce errors of measurement substantially and would be of considerable utility in borderline decisions. A Bayesian estimate of a candidate's status as passing or failing gains in accuracy through taking into account not only direct, but also collateral and prior evidence. In the case of Advanced level, the evidence would be respectively the candidate's raw mark in the examination, and also the marks achieved by other candidates from the same teaching group and the candidate's previous or current performance in other examinations or subjects.

Such a procedure might have appealed to HSC decision makers. In the current version of the German Abitur, which is a qualification of the HSC type, factors concerning the student's social background and method of preparing for the Abitur may be fed into the computer along with his grades on periodic and on terminal examinations in a group of subjects (Peterson, 1975). But there is only a remote likelihood that any board would introduce such a system into GCE decision making. The difference in potential acceptability is indicative of a shift in the frame of reference of GCE compared to HSC. GCE is without doubt referenced more to subjects than to candidates. Can one then assume that the operational definition of the HSC standard still holds good for the GCE system or have the chief examiners already reasserted their importance as carriers of standards within subjects across time?

4 Present Advanced-level grading practice in the JMB

The GCE boards have been charged with the maintenance of standards between subjects and over time. We have seen that they inherited a grading system whose appeal lay in its apparent efficacy in equating standards between subjects. We have also seen that the domain referencing of GCE subjects provides at least the potential for chief examiners to recognize fluctuations in standard over time. We have further seen that these two requirements, stability over subjects and stability over time, approximately coincide with two grading philosophies, norm-referenced and domain-referenced assessment. How far have these philosophies influenced current practice?

Curiously little information is available on this point. As long as no firm priorities have been established among the standards to be maintained and no hard and fast maintenance procedure has been laid down, a certain degree of confusion must linger. It is in the detail rather than the broad outlines of standardization procedures that crucial differences of emphasis inhere. For example, Petch characterizes the JMB as implementing a clear-cut strategy in 1953. The account which follows of current JMB grading practices is equally circumstantial. It is interpreted by the present secretariat as tending towards the implementation of an absolute, rather than an entry determined, standard.

THE JMB FINAL MEETING OF EXAMINERS

The research officers of the GCE boards have recently provided a schematic account of the procedures by which GCE boards arrive at their grade boundaries (Bardell *et al.*, 1978, p. 30). This does not depart in substance from the more extended account of the behaviour of JMB chief examiners to be found in Christie and Forrest (1980, Chapter 2). Throughout the GCE system the crucial step in the determination of grades, and hence standards, is the Final Meeting between chief examiners and senior administrative staff of the Board. The key role of the chief examiner as the carrier of standards from year to year was a fundamental assumption of the Christie and Forrest (1980) comparability study. While it was not the immediate focus of their research, their analysis of the chief examiner's behaviour gave rise to a statistical model which showed a good fit to the empirical data generated from JMB practice.

Each chief examiner of the JMB, in the light of his own first-instance marking, his review of samples of the marking of assistant examiners, the observations of assistants on the demands of the paper and the level of response of the candidates, submits a preliminary report to the Secretary. In this report a chief examiner gives his overall impressions of the demands of the paper and the quality of the responses as compared with those presented in the previous year in relation to

(a) the general standard of performance, and
(b) the standard of performance amongst the better candidates (i.e. those likely to achieve Grade B or above).

In addition, a chief examiner is asked to add any further comments which might be of value to the Secretary in estimating appropriate levels of performance for the review of scripts of the B/C, C/D and E/O borderlines. However, these are borderlines for the examination as a whole and a chief examiner is normally only responsible for one of the two or more papers of which most Advanced-level examinations consist.

In respect of that one paper he has much experience to draw upon. Even before becoming a chief examiner he will normally have taken part in the borderline review in which all scripts one or two marks below the critical borderlines are scrutinized. This is a lengthy process of anything from three to ten days' duration in the large entry subjects since the number of scripts involved can run into hundreds. It has the invaluable effect of ensuring that chief examiners have at least the opportunity to develop a sound intuitive grasp of the characteristics of borderline scripts if only through sheer repetition.

On this intuitive judgement alone the chief examiner must rely in making his preliminary recommendations. He has only seen responses to his paper. He does not have a distribution of the total marks for the examination on the basis of which the grades will be awarded. He does not have the information relating to the performance of candidates in the other components of the examination. He has only a layman's knowledge of standards in other subjects.

Members of the secretariat may be able to make an expert contribution to subject grading in their individual areas of interest but of course deal with a range of subjects so that they are almost always in the position of looking at standards in a subject from outside. In addition to the chief examiners' reports the secretariat has access to further information bearing on grade boundary decisions. Statistical data on the current examination, the previous few years' examinations and comparability with other subjects within the board are routinely available. Formal or informal information may also be available from studies of comparability with the same subject as examined by different boards and any observations which have implications for standards will have been abstracted from the records of the Board's Subject Committees or from the Schools Council scrutiny of the GCE boards' scripts.

The statistical data for the current year consist of computer print-outs of the distribution of marks for each examination component and the distribution of total marks. The data are based on adjusted marks, that is, the process of adding or subtracting marks to bring individual examiners more closely into line with general standards has already been carried out. For the previous year's examination parallel information is available together with the grade boundaries finally adopted plus summary data for previous years. Comparability between subjects in the previous year is provided in the JMB by the annual subject pairs comparisons (Joint Matriculation Board, 1975), which are based, like the distributions, on the total candidate entry.

When all this material has been collated it is dealt with by the Secretary, the one person who sees the information for each and every final examiners' meeting. In the light of all the information available the Secretary attempts to estimate the mark ranges within which the key grade boundaries (i.e. B/C, C/D and E/O) are likely to fall. The percentage norms suggested for the various grades at Advanced level (Secondary School Examinations Council, 1960) are an additional factor of which notice is taken, but primarily the process consists of comparing marks and awards in the subject in the previous year with the judgements of the examiners for the current year rather than the automatic application of the suggested percentage norms.

At each of the three key grade boundaries a small range of marks is selected to ensure that the necessary samples of scripts can be available when the chief examiners and secretariat meet at the Final Meeting. The secretariat action on the selection of scripts is not intended to influence the decision of the Final Meeting; the procedure is intended to save time which would be wasted if chief examiners had to wait for the samples of scripts to be identified and assembled.

At the Final Meeting the statistical data relating to the examination are presented to the chief examiners and the salient features are pointed out by the Secretary. It should be noted that, although each chief examiner will have a reasonably clear picture of what has happened in his own component, the Chairman of Examiners is normally the only person who has sampled work in all components; but even he will be seeing the statistical information relating to the examination as a whole for the first time.

The amount of discussion which takes place at the Final Meeting depends partly on the extent to which the subjective impressions recorded by the chief examiners in the preliminary reports are supported by the examination statistics and partly on the extent to which other factors (comparability reports, subject pairs comparisons, etc.) need to be taken into account. Following a consideration of these general issues, the Secretary explains the preliminary estimates he has made of the mark ranges at the key points from which samples of scripts have been assembled. As a result of the subsequent discussion three possibilities arise. It may be agreed that the mark ranges selected are appropriate, in which case the chief examiners review the scripts and reach decisions on the minimum marks for grades B, C and E. It may be agreed that one (or more) of the mark ranges selected by the Secretary needs extending[1]; in this situation more scripts need to be assembled so that the review to ascertain the minimum marks for the particular grades may proceed. This step was taken on five occasions in 1977 in 34 subjects (or alternatives within subjects) with an entry of more than 250 candidates. Exceptionally it may be agreed that one or more of the mark ranges selected is so inappropriate that a new mark range has to be chosen and new samples of scripts assembled before the review to determine minimum marks for the relevant grades can take place.

The other grade boundaries (A/B, D/E and allowed Ordinary/fail) are determined by the Secretary who is guided by the SSEC suggested percentage norms but also takes into account the run of marks as well as the position of the agreed key points so that, for example, if grades A and B together include more than the suggested 25 per cent of candidates, the A/B point will be fixed so as to place more than 10 per cent of the candidates in grade A. Although there are slight differences even within the JMB itself, the process varying in accordance with the nature of the examination and the various external factors involved, in general some grade boundaries (B/C, E/O and more recently C/D) are fixed by a process in which judgements of quality by the senior examiners play a direct part whereas, for the remaining grade boundaries (A/B, D/E and allowed Ordinary/fail),

1 For example, in 1976, in English Literature (Advanced) the mark ranges selected by the Secretary were

    B/C   105–111
    C/D   97–103
    E/O   76–82   (marks out of a total of 200)

During the course of the Final Meeting the chief examiners extended the mark ranges (upwards) so that additional scripts had to be obtained. The B/C range became 105–113, the C/D 97–104 and E/O 76–83. Thus scripts at all marks from 97 to 113 inclusive were sampled before the B/C and C/D points were agreed (at 110 and 104 marks respectively). Between 96 and 114 marks there were 3745 candidates, that is, 23 % of the total entry. Fewer candidates were allocated to grade C, or better than would have been the case had the original suggestions made by the Secretary remained unchanged.

the decisions are taken by the Secretary to reflect the expected percentage norms and qualitative decisions already reached.

From a research point of view it would be most instructive if the estimates of where the key points in a mark distribution lie were to be made independently of each other; that is to say, if the examiners were able to look at and consider scripts without reference to the overall mark distributions and if the Secretary were to base suggestions simply on statistical information. Any conflict of view would be more readily apparent. It would be possible to establish how often disagreements exist between standards defined by reference to quality of work (the contribution of the chief examiners) and standards defined in terms of distribution of candidates (the contribution of the Secretary). But in JMB practice at least, all available information is used by the Secretariat to anticipate the needs of examiners by ensuring that the scripts assembled in the likely regions of the key points are available with the minimum of delay.

A CONTEST MODEL OF THE IMPLEMENTATION OF STANDARDS

The foregoing account is of sweet reasonableness itself, the very epitome of that equilibrium which pre-war investigators signally failed to find. But the arrangements as described also allow of an outcome of a different complexion. The grade boundaries are a group decision and groups do not unfailingly make reasonable decisions. The participants sit down with somewhat different perspectives, different experience and different expertise and certainly not on equal terms to negotiate an agreement. If the statistical information coincides with subjective judgement the agreement will be quickly reached. But what might happen if there were an apparent conflict between the two kinds of evidence? Does the stronger personality win, as a cynic might conclude from the variations between subjects in the pattern of award over time? Or is there an identifiable pattern of compromise?

One circumstance which would lead to disagreement between the subjective judgements of examiners and the statistical evidence prepared by the secretariat is a gradual or abrupt change in the character of the entry. Such a change could come about in a variety of ways; an old subject might lose its status as a quasi-obligatory requirement for entry to a desired profession; a new subject might be staffed almost without exception by young and enthusiastic teachers eager for the posts of special responsibility only increased numbers can bring. Whatever the cause, it is possible to speculate that something like the following hypothetical course of events might have occurred:

It is a fact that in the 1960's Economics entries grew dramatically while Mathematics was at a standstill, effectively losing ground. Now if

Mathematics were losing a disproportionately large number of better candidates to Economics, the Mathematics examiners would wish to reduce the percentage of passing candidates. Conversely the Economics examiners would look for an increase. But what statistical information would there be to substantiate their claim? There might be a hesitation in the Mathematics growth curve, an acceleration in Economics, but no reason to connect the two. The only evidence of movement would be contingent changes in the raw mark distributions, probably not dramatic when only two adjacent years are under consideration. They would be as readily attributable to the scaling characteristics of this year's questions as to the calibre of this year's entry. In fact there is no empirical justification either for the choice of Economics in this hypothetical example as the resting place of the lost Mathematics candidates nor for the characterization of their aptitudes. On such statistical evidence the Secretary can only urge caution on his chief examiners in changing more than marginally the expectation of passing. A small compromise might be made. Yet successive small compromises could lead to a marked shift in standards.

5 Evidence from the outcomes of examiners' final meetings

Some empirical evidence can be brought to bear on these speculations about the social dynamics of final examiners' meetings from the data made available by JMB comparability studies. The argument involves the following three major assumptions.

(a) The chief examiners can indeed identify with some accuracy the standard associated with a borderline script. In 1953, Petch felt able to reply to those who 'posit the existence of absolute standards which are communicable from examiner to examiner, from panel to panel, passed as it were year by year from hand to hand like some foot-rule. If absolute standards do exist, they have never been revealed to the Board or to its examiners' (p. 147). However by 1973, and admittedly within stable panels of senior examiners in English Literature and more especially in Chemistry and Mathematics, members of the examining teams independently nominated marks within a very narrow range as being the borderline, even in the absence of a script or scripts on the nominated mark (Christie and Forrest, 1980). Moreover their marking was consonant with a model which made this assumption.

(b) The Secretary promotes a passing percentage which is closely based on the percentage pass in the previous year, or perhaps two years, if the passing percentage is beginning to diverge from the statistical norm in similar subjects. This was certainly the case in the JMB in 1953.

(c) The passing percentage endorsed by the final meeting is a compromise between the demands of comparability over time (the absolute standard of the examiners) and of comparability between subjects (the norm-based standard of the Secretary) and will fall somewhere between the passing percentage suggested by the examiners and that suggested by the Secretary.

It follows from these assumptions that in a subject which records a higher percentage passing than pass in similar cognate subjects there will have been pressure on the examiners by the Secretary to reduce the numbers passing, that is, to adopt a more severe standard. Conversely, in a subject where the examiners' initial position would pass relatively few candidates, they will have come under pressure to 'ease' their standard to allow a greater proportion of candidates to pass. Of course the published passing percentages cannot of themselves indicate whether compromise took place, but it is hypothesized that a significant positive association between severity of standard and a higher than normal percentage passing is the outcome of such a compromise and, by implication, evidence that examiners can carry a standard from year to year.

'Severity of standard' has been operationally defined by the JMB Advanced-level subject pairs comparisons. These belong to the family of techniques reviewed by Nuttall *et al.* (1974) and are subject to the weakness outlined above on page 9. They have the further infelicity of using the extent to which there is an equivalent expectation of achieving the average grade awarded in each pair of subjects, somewhere around the D/E borderline rather than the passing grade, the E/O borderline. On the other hand, in the version used for these analyses, the relatedness of subjects is reflected in the frequency with which any subject pair contributes to the overall index of severity thus mitigating the impact of the most important limiting assumption, that of a constant inter-subject correlation. Finally, and crucially in this analysis, subject pairs comparisons are independent both of the evidence which guides the decisions of examiners and of the evidence which guides the recommendations of the secretariat. Although the subject pairs comparison is based on the performance of all Advanced-level candidates in a given pair of subjects, and so makes no distinction between different types of subjects, the subjects here are split into three groups. There is overwhelming evidence ably reviewed by McVey (1978) for a greater apparent severity of grading in the science subjects, while Kelly (1976) is only the most recent researcher to express misgivings regarding the applicability of subject pairs or reference test techniques of standardization, both of which make an implicit single general ability assumption to subjects, especially Art, Domestic Science and Geometrical and Engineering Drawing, with a major performance component. The differences usually found among these groups were anticipated to be such as to swamp the effect we seek here and so the analysis is of differences in severity within allied subject groups. A 'normal' percentage passing has been operationally defined in Table 3 by ranking the percentages within allied groups of subjects, that is, the median passing percentage of the group becomes 'normal'.

Table 3 presents data relating to three groups of subjects. The hypothesized effect is clearly to be seen among the subjects classed as humanities. Neither of the other two groups shows a monotonic relationship. In the case of the performance-based subjects this is perhaps not surprising, since this is an essentially contrived grouping with no natural identity. The failure of the science group on the other hand must throw some doubt on the generality of this suggested conclusion, though, with hindsight, one might have predicted that it is in the non-science subjects, notorious for the difficulties in assessment that they engender, that the examiners would feel least secure in their judgements and that evidence of compromise would be most readily obtained. It is worth noting in this respect that, if the comparability index in Table 3 is adjusted to yield a mean of zero within each group of subjects, then there is overall a significant relationship (Yule's $Q = 0.35$) between severity and a passing percentage in excess of the SSEC recommended 70 per cent.

Evidence that there is a compromise between the examiner's judgement of a standard of attainment and the statistical norms relating to standardization of opportunity, while by no means clear cut from these data, cannot be lightly dismissed, especially as it is not contended that a compromise will always be called for. Indeed the general satisfaction within GCE boards with the procedures of the examiners' final meeting rather suggests that in most subjects there is little conflict between and even a comforting

Table 3   Passing percentages in 1973 JMB Advanced-level subjects and severity relative to all other Advanced levels presented in conjunction with the subject

Subject	Percentage awarded Grade E or better	Severity[1]
Humanities		
Greek	92·7	0·8
Latin	79·4	0·8
Russian	78·0	0·4
Spanish	76·9	0·0
German	75·5	0·3
English Literature	72·0	− 0·5
French	71·0	0·3
Geography	69·8	− 0·6
History	68·4	0·0
Economics	68·4	− 0·5
British Constitution	68·4	− 0·5
Religious Knowledge	68·4	− 0·5

tau $= 0.65$, $z = 2.60$, $p < 0.01$

Table 3 (*continued*)

Subject	Percentage awarded Grade E or better	Severity[1]
Sciences		
Further Mathematics	76·9	1·1
Physics	73·4	0·5
Geology	71·8	−0·8
Chemistry	71·5	−0·1
Biology	68·0	0·2
Pure Mathematics	67·3	0·5
Mathematics	65·9	0·6
Pure Mathematics with Statistics	52·7	1·0
tau = 0·25, z = 0·75, not significant		
Performance-based subjects		
Art	77·9	−1·1
Music	76·8	−1·4
Metalwork	75·2	−1·0
Geometrical and Engineering Drawing	70·7	−0·7
Woodwork	65·9	−0·9
Craft (Design and Practice)	62·3	−0·2
Domestic Science (Needlework)	53·4	−1·1
Domestic Science (The Home, the Family and Society)	49·9	0·0
tau = −0·33, z = 0·99, not significant		

[1] Severity is operationalized as the difference between the mean grade in the named subject and the unweighted mean in the other subjects offered by the named subject candidates: a positive difference indicates severity.

coincidence of the two sets of evidence. Every such agreement will weaken the observed relationship.

Given these considerations, it seems fair to draw the following conclusions:

(a) Chief examiners are capable of carrying a standard from year to year.
(b) Conflicts can arise between the requirement of maintaining stable standards of attainment over time and the requirement of maintaining a probability of obtaining a pass which is comparable with that in other subjects.

The second conclusion is amenable to direct test. One of the recommendations for the conduct of future studies of comparability of standards over time (Christie and Forrest, 1980, Appendix A) is that very full records of the transactions in Final Meetings be kept: a study of these should throw more light on this aspect of grading procedures.

CHANGES IN SUBJECT POPULARITY AND RELATIVE SEVERITY

A further demonstration of the extent, if any, of tension between the demands of comparability over time and comparability between subjects is possible. The most probable circumstance which might bring about a conflict between the two criteria is when increases and decreases in the relative popularity of subjects arise from the movement of groups of candidates which are unrepresentative in respect of their academic ability.

Such effects are most likely to be seen in subjects which are either failing to hold their accustomed proportion of the Advanced-level entry or alternatively are increasing their proportional share, presumably by recruiting candidates from the first group of subjects. Taking changes in relative severity over time as the independent variable, Table 4 sets out the consequences for the relative popularity of subjects.

The subject pairs comparisons for 1973 are again the index of severity in Table 4. The status of each subject's market share has been determined from Table 8 of the Joint Matriculation Board's *Seventieth Annual Report* (1973). Subjects with a falling share have been defined as those which suffered a reduction in the actual number of entries between 1966, the earliest year reported in that table, and 1973. Subjects with a rising share have been defined as those whose percentage of total Advanced-level entries increased. Subjects falling in neither category, that is with increasing numbers but a falling percentage share of the market, have been defined as stable. (If any year earlier than 1966 is taken as the baseline, the number of subjects in the three groups becomes very unequal due to the small absolute numbers of subject entries before that date.)

The results in Table 4 are unusually clear cut. Every one of the subjects in which the number of entries is reducing is classed by the subject pairs comparison as tending towards severity ($p < 0.005$, binomial theorem). Similarly subjects attracting an increasing share of the market are for the most part lenient. Biology is the only undoubted exception to that generalization, since both Pure Mathematics and Pure Mathematics with Statistics share a common paper with Mathematics Syllabus A and their grade boundaries are to a considerable extent dependent on the decisions arrived at in the parent subject. Excluding these two mathematics subjects from consideration, the changing popularity of subjects accounts for 63 per cent of the variation in standard between subjects ($F = 12.94$ with 2, 18 d.f.). Changes in popularity lead to highly systematic distortions of grade boundary decisions.

Table 4 Relation of severity of standard relative to other JMB Advanced-level subjects in 1973 to change in popularity since 1966

Share down	Severity	Share up	Severity	Stable	Severity
Greek	0·8	English Literature	−0·5	Spanish	0·0
Latin	0·8	Geography	−0·6	History	0·0
German	0·3	Economics	−0·5	Religious Knowledge	−0·5
French	0·3	British Constitution	−05	Physics	0·5
Further Maths	1·1	Geology	−0·8	Chemistry	−0·1
Maths	0·6	Biology	0·2	Art	−1·1
		Music	−1·4		
		Geometrical & Engineering Drawing	−0·7		
		Domestic Science (The Home, the Family and Society)	0·0		
		Pure Maths	0·5		
		Pure Maths with Statistics	1·0		

Unfortunately the results cannot reveal how it has come about that subjects whose popularity is declining are more severe in the standards they set. There are at least three possibilities. Explanation A is that the relative lenience or severity of grading in the various subjects has led to changes in their popularity. Duckworth and Entwistle (1974) report that there is considerable agreement among pupils in their perceptions of which subjects are difficult. By the fifth form, boys and girls agreed in ranking the difficult subjects as Physics, Chemistry, Latin and Mathematics in that order. French was seen as difficult by second form boys. The concordance of that list with the list of subjects in Table 4 whose share of the Advanced-level market has fallen is strong enough to suggest that pupils act upon their perceptions of subject difficulty in making Advanced-level course choices. Indeed Ormerod and Duckworth (1975), on the basis of ten British and three U.S. investigations, came to the conclusion that the difficulty of the subject area is the main cause of the flight from the physical sciences.

However, a note of caution must be entered. Both Physics and Chemistry are stable in Table 4 and Chemistry at least is not unduly severe. Unfortunately we have no data relevant to the upswing in popularity of science subjects during the 1950's (subject pairs comparisons were not made prior to 1972) and the current change in trend is not yet sufficiently mature to allow comparison. Relative severity of grading as a cause of changes in subject popularity is an attractive but merely plausible hypothesis. To accept explanation A as a sufficient account of the pattern of Table 4 is simply to discount Table 4 as evidence bearing upon the contest model of grading decisions.

The other two possibilities assume that changes in popularity lead to lenience or severity in grading. They are contingent upon the transactions in the examiners' final meetings. On the one hand (explanation B), it may be that movements between subjects are made by candidates of no particular aptitude, or commitment, or both, so that those who remain in a subject of falling popularity are a more than usually talented group. If this is the case, the results are entirely consonant with the model proposed in the first study (p. 39 above) in which examiners propose an absolute standard which would pass some extreme percentage of candidates and the board secretariat forces a compromise. On the other hand (explanation C), it may be that the examiners act in accordance with a prejudice which they bring to the situation rather than in the light of the evidence as they have seen it. If the examiners are convinced that quality and quantity in so far as they apply to subject entries are inversely related, they may base their argument for an extreme passing percentage not on the evidence of an absolute standard but on the basis of a hunch that the reduced numbers of candidates must be better or —and this more familiar argument would produce entirely the same result—that the vastly increased candidate entry must be worse.

Some light is thrown on these alternative explanations by the behaviour of the English Literature examiners in the Christie and Forrest (1980) study, who while producing a written report lamenting the obvious drop in standards since 1963, nominated a standard which was in effect slightly more severe than that obtaining in that golden age. Their perceptions of the crucial scripts (and of which scripts were crucial) were highly accurate, while their perceptions of the overall distribution and its implications were quite aberrant. Thus their crucial activities as examiners conformed to the expectations of explanation B but their public pronouncements—essentially as lay persons since they had no access to overall distributions of marks—conformed to explanation C. Such behaviour is entirely in accord with the contest model of GCE grading practice.

THE CHANGING CALIBRE OF CANDIDATES IN LENIENT AND SEVERE SUBJECTS

The most plausible of the possible explanations, that traditional subjects in decline retain only their strongest candidates while weaker students move elsewhere, is open to direct test using Ordinary-level results as the index of candidate calibre. To allow of cross reference to the Christie and Forrest study of comparability of standards over time, 1963 and 1973 are the comparison years and English Literature is taken as representative of the subjects maintaining their popularity, while Mathematics and Chemistry represent subjects which are losing popularity and remaining stable respectively. In each subject and year a random sample of 100 candidates was drawn from the Advanced-level broadsheets[1] and their grades recorded. The Ordinary-level broadsheets for two years earlier were then consulted and the Ordinary-level results of the sampled candidates recorded. As the grading scheme at Ordinary level was different in 1961 from that in use in 1971, each subject attempted was simply recorded as pass or fail. Any candidate who had attempted fewer than four Ordinary levels in the year consulted was assumed to be a resit candidate at either Ordinary or Advanced level and replaced in the sample.

The average numbers of Ordinary-level successes and failures for candidates at each Advanced grade level in each subject and each year are reported in Appendix C. It may be seen from Appendix C that in each year the average number of subjects entered is approximately constant but with the number of passes and fails enjoying a reciprocal relationship across grade levels. The average number of O-levels passed at each grade level of

---

1 Broadsheets consist of the grades of individual candidates within each centre, the centres arranged in order.

each subject in each year has been taken as the dependent variable in a three-way analysis of variance reported in Table 5. The focus of attention is the subject-by-year interaction which indicates whether there is any significant difference between the subjects in the amount of change over time in the Ordinary-level calibre of their candidates. The analysis indicates that there is, and the appropriate mean values are set out in Table 6. As these means are based on an unweighted composite their absolute magnitudes are likely to be somewhat misleading and only their relative magnitude is of note. The number of passing performances at Ordinary level of Advanced-level English Literature candidates is the same in both years. The change in Chemistry, chosen as a 'stable', that is, marginally declining subject, is on the borderline of significance for a two-tailed test ($t = 2.18$ with 12 d.f. for $p < 0.05$). The number of Ordinary levels passed by candidates in Mathematics, which in 1973 had a much reduced entry, show a marked increase. The notion that a subject suffering a decline in popularity nevertheless retains its better candidates is vindicated.

THE VALIDITY OF THE CONTEST MODEL

The three empirical studies, taken as a group, support the inferred contest model of Advanced-level grading. In the contest model, gradual changes in the nature of the entry bring about a tension in most subjects between the secretariat intent on maintaining comparability between subjects by reference to an expectation of passing and the examiners who, by their concern with the actual quality of borderline scripts, act to maintain continuity of standards between years. The conflict in the contest model of

Table 5   Analysis of variance in the average number of Ordinary-level passes held by candidates at each Advanced-level grade in JMB English Literature, Mathematics and Chemistry in 1963 and 1973

Source	Sums of squares	d.f.	Mean square	F	Significance
Subjects(s)	7·0658	2	3·5329		
Years(y)	2·4240	1	2·4240		
Grades(g)	31·1154	6	5·1859	20·92	$p < 0.01$
s ×y	2·5496	2	1·2748	5·14	$p < 0.025$
s ×g	4·5396	12	0·3783	1·53	n.s.
y ×g	3·1354	6	0·5226	2·11	n.s.
s ×y ×g	2·9743	12	0·2479		
Total	53·8041	41	—		

Table 6 Unweighted average of Ordinary-level successes achieved by a random sample of candidates in JMB Advanced-level English Literature, Mathematics and Chemistry in 1963 and 1973

Subject	Means		Difference	t	Significance
	1963	1973			
English Literature	5·75	5·59	− 0·16	1·0	n.s.
Mathematics	5·90	6·94	1·04	3·91	$p < 0.01$
Chemistry	6·35	6·91	0·56	2·11	n.s.

Advanced-level grading is one between competing frames of reference by which standards can be held to have been maintained.

But, while the results of the three empirical studies reported here are quite consistent with each other, they are a direct reversal of those reported by Christie and Forrest (1980). In their study of comparability of standards at Advanced-level between 1963 and 1973, Mathematics standards eased considerably at the pass/fail borderline but not at the B/C borderline. In Chemistry the same trend in results may have been present but was masked by a massive syllabus change. English Literature showed no apparent change in standard but the unreliability inherent in the procedures of assessing English Literature was such that only dramatic shifts in the quality of response could have reached statistical significance: the direction of shift was towards a more severe requirement in 1973. These results are apparently at variance with the 1973 subject pairs comparison of the relative standards of subjects (Mathematics and Chemistry severe; English Literature lenient) and with the relatively more select candidate entry in Mathematics in 1973 than in 1963. (Indeed, the authors were led to hypothesize in Christie and Forrest (1980) that it was in fact bright, not mediocre, Advanced-level candidates who made the shift from declining to recruiting Advanced-level subjects.)

The contradiction is more apparent than real. If Advanced-level results are affected by the changing nature and size of the entry, will not Ordinary-level results suffer the same fate? Changes in the size of Ordinary-level entries have been much more exaggerated than at Advanced level, and so the relationship of six Ordinary-level passes in 1973 to five Ordinary-level passes in 1963 is a matter of conjecture. The uncertainties of Ordinary-level grading procedures could turn the results on their heads.

Alternatively, one may suppose that the 'reference tests' used in these empirical studies—performance at Ordinary level, performance in other Advanced-level subjects— are an accurate reflection of academic aptitude.

When aptitude goes up or down, does the actual quality of student work in the classroom increase or decrease? Reporting on several hundred American colleges, Baird and Feister (1972) conclude:

> . . . taken as aggregate groups, faculties *tended* to award a broader range of grades [in response to a more heterogeneous entry]. These tendencies were moderate, however [Correlations ranging around $r = 0.4$]. Most of the variance in the means and standard deviations of college grades were (sic) unrelated to the means and standard deviations of student talent (p. 5).

Such modest relationships will come as no surprise to those familiar with attempts to show an effect on achievement of streaming by ability. Dahllöf (1971) provides an attractive hypothesis to explain the very weak relationship between aptitude and classroom achievement. He identifies the crucial pedagogical decision as the decision to move on to a new syllabus element and claims that, in Sweden and probably in Ohio, teachers take as their touchstone of class readiness the state of knowledge of the pupil who is about three-quarters of the way down the rank order in the class. That pupil fixes the rate of progress for the class and any changes in aptitude which leave the bottom quarter of the class relatively unaffected will have no impact on the rate of progress through the syllabus and hence probably on the cumulative achievement of the group (Bennett, 1978). This key candidate will tend in the sixth form to be the borderline Advanced-level pass candidate. It is unlikely therefore that the phenomenon is confined to Sweden.

The relationship between aptitude and achievement in the classroom setting is by no means clear cut and relatively little is known of how the relationship is mediated. This paucity of cogent analysis may be due in some measure to the lack of a clear-cut criterion of educational achievement. Public examination grades as currently conceived reflect both aptitude and attainment: they represent both the cause and the effect of educational achievement.

In sum, there is no compelling reason why analyses of concurrent standards using a latent-trait or general ability assumption (the subject pairs comparisons) should concur with analyses of standards carried over time which use a judgemental approach to 'things known' (Christie and Forrest, 1980). The two kinds of standard are conceptually distinct. They have different frames of reference and the processes by which they are arrived at are quite independent of each other. Add in the pervasive 70 per cent passing expectation, which is independent both of parity over time and of parity between subjects, and confusion is increased. What is clear, however, is that until some definite conclusion is reached on which kind of standard is to be maintained the educational planner will be denied information about, for instance, changes in the characteristics of the sixth form population, which is fundamental to the provision of sixth form education.

The final picture is of competition rather than of equilibrium between the dual functions of measuring achievement at a given point in time and providing for selection for further study. The maintenance of standards has evolved within the GCE system as a corporate responsibility. From the outside it looks an uneasy amalgam of potentially competing considerations. The maintenance of comparability of an achievement level over time (the borderline recommendations of the chief examiners), of a percentage expectation of success over time (last year's distributions) and of comparability between subjects (the subject pairs comparisons) can all at one time or another quite legitimately become the most salient consideration in deciding the precise mark to be a grade boundary. GCE boards, CSE boards and working parties charged with designing examinations for the common 16 + system can hardly be expected to maintain 'standards' until the standards to be maintained are more completely specified and an order of priority established among them.

6 The grading scheme as frame of reference

The question of priorities among the standards that might be maintained is essentially a question about the definition of the grading scheme. The crucial aspect of a grading scheme is not the number of grades but a decision about anchor points. Any grade or mark, even though every effort has been made to ensure it is a valid estimate of competence in the subject, still begs the question, 'With respect to what frame of reference is this competence expressed?' The frame of reference may be performance by all candidates in all subjects at the appropriate level, and incidentally norm-referenced, or it may be the performance of particular candidates in the specified subject in previous years and incidentally criterion-referenced in that agreed achievement criteria for the subject are implicit in the selection of candidates.

The traditional frame of reference of the public examination system is the latent trait model of classical psychometric theory. This approach was developed at the turn of the century to cope with a particular problem, the measurement of intelligence, but is readily generalizable to any situation where what is to be measured is an open concept without a finite set of defining attributes. The technique of identification depends upon two guiding assumptions, that when many discrete behaviours covary they have a single cause or determinant and that different behavers are possessed of more or less of this determinant, allowing them to be located at equal intervals along a metaphysical measuring stick.[1] Derived from these assumptions are all the technical paraphernalia of standardized test

---

1 Few are more metaphysical than that suggested by Rasch (1960) and applied in the educational context by Willmott and Fowles (1974). For a critical assessment of its potential utility see Wood, (1976(b)) and especially Goldstein (1979) who notes: 'the essence of many educational systems is the diversity of approaches whose actual aim to create differential attainments among otherwise similar children, for example . . . as a result of different pedagogical objectives. While this situation need not rule out the possibility of a single common assessment, it does seem to be at odds with the rationale underlying the Rasch model and, by extension, other unidimensional latent trait models.' (p. 217)

construction—facility and discrimination values, norm tables and above all the internal consistency coefficient. The latter measures the extent to which each item correlates with every other item and so, the higher the internal consistency coefficient, the closer the interrelationships among the items and the stronger the presumption of a single underlying causal determinant—a latent trait. But there is a price to be paid in return for this assumption—the absolute necessity of construct validation. Construct validation is required since, although the resulting test can be treated as if the behaviours it involves have a single determinant, the characteristics of that determinant (construct), and thus its identification, are still matters of doubt. For example, Atkinson (1974) can point out without unwarranted exaggeration:

Until proven otherwise, any measured difference in what has been called general intelligence, scholastic aptitude, verbal or mathematical ability, etc., which is always obtained from performance under achievement-oriented if not multiple-incentive conditions, can be given a motivational interpretation with no less scientific justification than the traditional aptitudinal interpretation. (p. 395)

Protagonists of the criterion-referenced approach to educational measurement tend to assume that it does not suffer this validity weakness and that none of the technical procedures is necessary since the characteristics of the construct are finite and listed in a domain specification which becomes a contract between examiner and candidate. Anything in the syllabus is fair game: anything not specified or not implied by something specified cannot be asked. If it is assumed that the thing achieved and the syllabus are one and the same, the necessity of construct validation disappears.

But Messick's (1975) counter to this happy state of affairs does in fact hold good. Although educational achievement tests are less dependent on hypothetical consistency of process than are most psychological tests, there are real problems about the generalizability of the contents of syllabuses. The moment that there are many different Advanced-level syllabuses with the same subject name content representativeness, that is of comparability of content, between alternative syllabuses as well as between boards, becomes an issue and only construct validation, the determination of what is properly to be understood by reference to that subject name, can resolve the issue.[1]

One can, however, accept Messick's stricture without having to accept either the technical paraphernalia or the full-blown latent trait model. The adequacy of the model in the personality domain, where it is encapsulated in such personality 'dimensions' as neuroticism or anxiety, is currently

1   A move in this direction may be seen in the requirement that in the common system of examining at 16 + subject criteria are to be laid down which must be met before the name of the subject can be used to refer to the syllabus.

under challenge. It appears to be insufficient, in itself, to account for behaviour of any complexity, even the behaviour involved in taking personality tests (Argyle, 1976). Alternative formulations in terms of specific short-lived states rather than generalized traits are proving to have considerable explanatory power (cf. Spielberger, 1972) and one current focus of research is on the mechanism by which eliciting situations recur with sufficient frequency to create behavioural consistency (Magnusson and Endler, 1977), that is, the appearance of a trait.

Even in the area of the first great triumph of the psychometric movement, general intelligence objectively determined and measured, the latent trait model has always been open to challenge. Spearman (1927) was responsible for one of the first trait formulations; he attributed school subject achievements to just two explanatory concepts, subject aptitude and 'g'. That model has been highly influential. Kelly (1976) in her study of comparability of standards between subjects finds on the basis of her factor analysis of between-subject correlations that 'the concept of general ability underlying examination performance is tenable for academic subjects but is much more dubious for non-academic subjects' (p. 57). Not for the first time, the potency of the notion triumphs over the pattern of the data.

In fact, Spearman's theory was early recognized as by no means the only possible explanation of his own data. The tendency towards positive correlations between different achievements is also entirely compatible with Sir Godfrey Thomson's (1939) 'Sampling theory of Bonds'. He rejects the notion that 'g' is sufficient proof of a faculty or power of the mind. Were the mind held to consist of a large number of 'bonds'—inherited reflexes, common associations, acquired habits, the vast conglomerate of separate learning experiences that represent cultural membership—and if any intellectual test sampled a large number of these bonds the same pattern of correlations would emerge. The bonds are not necessarily atomistic nor summative in their conjoint action. Abilities will vary markedly in their 'richness', some needing very many bonds some only few. But the sampling theory, if it is to account for the observed correlations, does require 'some approach to an "all-or-none" reaction in the bonds; that is, it supposes that a bond tends either not to come into the pattern at all, or to do so with its full force.' (p. 278). The theory agrees well with Thorndike's (1926) Quantity Hypothesis of intelligence—that one mind is more intelligent than another simply because it possesses more interconnections out of which it can make patterns. Thomson concludes that the pattern of intercorrelations among aptitude and achievement tests

enables one to say that the mind works *as if* it were composed of a smallish number of common faculties *and a host of specific abilities*; but the phenomenon really arises from the fact that the mind is, compared with the body, so Protean and plastic, so lacking in separate and specialized organs . . . especially before education, language, the subjects of the school curriculum . . . have imposed a habitual structure on it. . . . Further, it is improbable that the organization of each mind is the same. The phrase, 'factors of *the* mind' suggests too strongly that this is so, and that minds differ only in the amount of each factor they possess. It is more than likely that different minds perform any task or test by different means, and indeed that the same mind does so at different times (1939, pp. 268–284 *passim*).

This much more cautious interactive interpretation not only accords well with the current position in personality theory, but the final sentence can be taken to summarize all that we know at present about examination performance.

The sampling theory does not preclude a ranking of individuals along some dimension but it does not presuppose it, and quite explicitly denies that there is a finite set of independent dimensions upon which ranking must take place. In that respect it is in the mainstream of a European psychological tradition which runs through the work of the Gestalt psychologists on perception, Sir Fred Bartlett (1932) on memory and culminates in Piaget's (1971) view of the origins of intelligence which is premised on the notion that knowledge is not a simple copy of reality but rather that knowledge is a consequence of activity. It follows in Piaget's epistemology that knowledge is not a general, coherent, and consistent picture of reality, independent of purposes and independent in the form in which it is represented. Each form of activity may be expected to yield a somewhat different form of knowledge. These forms of knowledge are schemata, 'an idea whose time has finally come' (Anderson, 1977, p. 416) to the United States!

. . . the implication of schema theory is that the neural representations which are used during perception and comprehension, and which evolve as a result of these processes, have a holistic character which cannot be understood as simple functions of their constituents (op. cit., p. 418).

Under the influence of information processing theories a re-evaluation is beginning to emerge in the transatlantic psychometric tradition of the abilities construct as the basis of individual differences (Carroll, 1976; Estes, 1974; Hunt, 1971). The field of educational measurement is also in a ferment through the impact of the criterion-referenced testing movement but as the initial impetus came from what was essentially a pedagogical tactic 'Mastery learning' (cf. Bloom *et al.*, 1971; Block, 1971) rather than a theoretical reorientation, much of the debate has remained at the level of technology—'arid statistics' (Wood, 1976(a)). Criterion-referenced measurement suffers in Wood's view 'from being so closely tied to test content'. He feels with Messick (1975) that all measurement should be 'construct referenced . . . an estimate of how much of something an individual displays or possesses, so that the basic question is "What is the nature of that something?" ' (op. cit., p. 71).

That the question remains unanswered may be attributed at least in part to the premature closure involved in a too ready espousal of the latent trait model in educational measurement. An alternative, much less constricting, model is available in the sampling theory of bonds. It does not posit, anticipate or require that behaviours within any domain of achievement should be homogeneous, nor that there is any necessary order of difficulty among different attainments. Indeed, its closest approximation to hierarchy, the notion of 'richness', allows of the same ambivalent relation of superordinate conceptual structures ('synthesis' in Bloom's (1956) process categorization) to task difficulty, as is frequently noted in studies of educational achievement. Seddon (1978), for instance, in his review of researches attempting to equate the levels of Bloom's taxonomy of educational objectives with task difficulty, notes the relative 'easiness' of the second highest level of categorization, synthesis. Perhaps this is only empirical verification that schema which are unusually rich in the number of 'bonds' involved will allow of a diversity of approaches to their understanding: presumably it was some such feature that Bruner (1960) had in mind in his famous dictum that there is an intellectually respectable way of teaching any concept to children at any age level. At the later stages of education, after years of research in which the arts man always emerged as merely the equal of his science contemporary in verbal ability, and much his inferior in numerical ability (for example, Choppin *et al.*, 1972; Christie and Mills, 1973) progress is finally being made in identifying a compensating accomplishment—one which, significantly enough, is rather difficult to scale as if it were a latent trait. It appears that a liberal arts education enhances the facility with which the student can form complex higher order conceptual structures from unordered, non-quantified information (Schroder *et al.*, 1967; Winter and McClelland, 1978). Pask (1976) in this country may have identified the same characteristic in the group he identifies as holists on the basis of their tendency to make more complex hypotheses while learning (though it could be that the authors are simply suffering from the pathology frequently associated with the holist learning style—globe-trotting, the making of inappropriate ideational links).

Suffice it to say that the sampling theory of bonds has considerable integrative power. It sits well with the initial outcomes of the determined onslaught being mounted on the topic of learning styles by Pask and his associates. They conclude that the valid analogies which promote rapid assimilation of meaningful data are often of a much more complex, idiosyncratic type than is suggested by most material analogies of the formal structure of the mind. It is also becoming clear to them that there are a variety of equally valid 'entailment meshes' (loosely, sequences of instruction) which will stand as analogies of method in representations of knowledge structures. The vocabulary is their own but there is broad agreement with Thomson's position.

More to the point, either formulation offers a ready explanation of the very moderate fit of the latent trait model to educational achievement. McIntyre and Brown (1978) report as the characteristic outcome of factor analyses of achievement tests:

Not only is the variation in performance on any one attainment test commonly describable only in terms of a considerable number of dimensions, but those dimensions are likely to be interpretable, if at all, only in terms of the specific *content* of the test items. (p. 45, our italics)

The same outcome may be viewed through trait-coloured glasses.

All data obtained during the educational testing process were held to be multitrait in nature, and this fact was thought to constitute the major reason for confusion over the meaning of experimental results derived from test data. It was considered that clarity of objective had been an overemphasized, but under-applied, concept. (Sumner, 1977, p. 271)

IMPLICATIONS FOR GRADING PROCEDURES

The reporting of norm-referenced single continuum grades assumed to be monotonically related to some underlying latent trait—whether it be academic aptitude, verbal aptitude or aptitude in answering questions about the Partition of Poland—is suspect not because it never fits the behaviour of candidates but only because it does not always fit the behaviour of candidates. Selectors choose to treat subjects as ready substitutes for each other—a survival into the specialized sixth form of the old ideal of a general education—and so the boards, in their grading practices, have felt compelled to treat all subjects as though they were similarly structured. The present Advanced-level grading practice assumes that the grades are best arrived at by a simple summation of the constituent elements of the performance, without regard to how disparate these constituents might be.

To this day in the JMB the situation noted by Crofts and Jones (1928) is current (see p. 18). The Advanced-level Mathematics examination produces an approximately rectangular mark distribution, ranging from 0 to almost 200 out of 200. Every year the English Literature examination produces a curious pear-shaped distribution in which a very large proportion of candidates occupies a very small proportion of the mark range (see above, p. 33 footnote). Every year, judging from the number of appeals against grades, the Mathematics examiners get it right and the English Literature examiners get it rather less right. The orthodox explanation is firmly bedded in latent trait theory. The Mathematics examination is reliable (or more precisely, internally consistent) and the English Literature examination is not. But whenever these subjects are examined and the total marks are an unweighted composite of a series of small decision points the outcome is the same whether at 11 + or at undergraduate level. Is English Literature then an unreliable subject?

The incongruity of the question is sufficient indication of the extent to which the latent trait model is over-generalized. There appears to be every reason to suppose that the subject matter of Mathematics is differently structured from the subject matter of English Literature, both in fact and intention. The objectives of a Mathematics course can be listed, itemized and cast in behavioural terms. The objectives of a course in English Literature tend to be couched in the language of religion, exalted, universalistic, invoking the ultimate values which cannot be defined but can be felt and attested to. Independent assessment of independent performances will produce the most reliable result, if there is a single latent trait in operation. But in English Literature a more valid result might ensue if one examiner were to read the entire examination output of a candidate to establish the presence or absence of any of an array of indicators. That one can anticipate a more valid result from a theoretically less valid measure is indicative of the inadequacy of our present theory of examination performance. If the lockstep of between-subject comparability were to be relaxed, examiners in the different subjects would be free to devise systems of assessment more closely referenced to the structure of their subjects. This is the appropriate sense in which public examination boards should regard domain-referenced measurement.

TYPES OF DOMAIN-REFERENCED MEASUREMENT

Meskanskas (1976), in a valuable review article, has identified three approaches to standard setting in domain-referenced measurement. All require that the syllabus provides a tight specification of the subject area but are quite unlike in their definition of mastery. One group does not define implicitly or explicitly the nature of mastery and is not worthy of further consideration. The other two approaches espouse respectively a continuum or a state model, and closely mirror the distinction made here between trait and bond sampling approaches.

Continuum models assume that mastery refers to a continuously distributed ability or set of abilities. Specific points on the continuum are identified with particular levels of competence and the individual's performance is then classified according to the regions of the scale: a grade C candidate equals or exceeds the lower bound for grade C but has not attained the aggregate required for grade B. Clearly grades issued on this basis would be entirely compatible with those issued at present. In subjects espousing this model it might not even be necessary to modify the examination, though the inclusion of a large number of questions, preferably in multiple choice format, would be an advantage in that the regions could be defined using Nedelsky's (1954) minimum pass level method. That method simply formalizes and structures the judgements which examiners currently make in carrying the standard from year to year. All that is required to move to this type of domain-referenced assessment in an Advanced-level subject is freedom to ignore standards in other subjects and the setting of one's own criteria for grade boundaries in advance. Something very like it is possibly already in operation in some high prestige subjects with very fierce chief examiners.

The continuum model will be particularly useful in subjects where it is felt that the learner undergoes a smooth progression from lower to higher proficiency levels, in which case it may not make sense to conceptualize a 100 per cent level of performance. The state model, the other alternative considered by Meskanskas, would be more appropriate to stage models of learning of the type with which Piaget has made us familiar, or to hierarchical sets of learning tasks such as conceptualized by Gagné (1962) in which an incomplete grasp at one level tends to ensure failure at another. In the state model true-score performance is viewed as an all-or-none performance on a dichotomous task; the standard or cutting score is intrinsic to the nature of the task. There will usually be a task to represent each facet or attribute of the state which is to be certificated—the defining attribute—and failure in one task will not normally be compensatable by an outstanding performance elsewhere. In current Advanced-level nomenclature a state model examination would involve 'hurdles', specified and particularized accomplishments regarded as a *sine qua non* to particular grade awards and should in theory imply profile reporting of results. Emrick's (1971) mastery learning evaluation model provides a suitable strategy for standard setting but, in effect, setting the examination is setting the standard in this model.

Clearly the state model represents a much more dramatic shift from the generality of practice in public examinations in the UK. Most notably, in a domain-referenced grading system which assumes a state model, the number of grades identified will be a function of the structure of the subject and may therefore differ between subjects.

OUTLINE OF A STATE-REFERENCED EXAMINATION

The state-referenced examination is the one usually implied in discussions of domain-referenced testing, and as it is the further from our present experience it is perhaps worthwhile to give a concrete example of how it might work. Modern language competence in the first five years of secondary school is seen by HM Inspectorate to involve mastery of four skills: reading, writing, speaking and listening. HM Inspectorate have itemized levels of competence in these skills which might typify the average modern language student after three years and after five years of secondary schooling (Department of Education and Science, 1978(c), Appendix). That analysis might be used as a starting point for an examination in the common system at 16+.

There are two points of note here. Some commentators seem to feel that the appeal to three-year and five-year 'norms' invalidates the entire domain-referenced approach. This is simply to confuse age norms with developmental norms: certainly the domain specification during the process of secondary schooling has to represent a realistic set of expectations, but for reasons quite extraneous to the measurement approach. Secondly, this example was chosen precisely because of the tight specification in the HMI's outline. As noted earlier, any domain-referenced system requires close specification of the domain which necessarily implies a closer effective control of the transactions in the classroom. Such control will not be welcomed and there is likely to be a much more active interest taken in the credentials of subject committees.

In a norm-referenced test of a syllabus modelled on the HMI's analysis of the desirable levels of skill acquisition one or more questions would be set to test each of the four skills, or if one of the skills should prove difficult or expensive to examine, it might be felt that the candidates' status in that respect could be inferred from the other questions. As there would probably be a choice of question, all questions would be marked out of the same total, a convenient round number greater than ten and less than thirty. In a domain referenced examination, eight questions would be set, one on each skill at each level of demand, with the higher level of demand attracting greater credit. Candidates could present themselves in all questions or in that allowed subset of questions where they felt moderately confident of success (self-administered tailored testing). There is thus little in the way of a dramatic change of format in a domain-referenced modern language examination. That conclusion would apply in a sufficient number of subjects to lead Popham and Husek (1969, p. 2) to the conclusion that: 'it is not possible to tell a norm-referenced test from a criterion-referenced test by looking at it.'

Consideration of the mark scheme would leave one in no doubt. All domain-referenced tests would have mark schemes and passing levels finalized at the same time as the examination paper. State-referenced mark schemes would display further differences. In a norm-referenced, and in some continuum-referenced mark schemes, the marks are summed regardless of their origin to arrive at a total which must exceed some lower bound, say 35 per cent. That criterion could be met either by candidates who could do nothing well but managed to avoid a signally bad performance on any of the questions they attempted, or by candidates who were highly competent in one or two aspects of the syllabus requirements and innocent of the others[1]. In a state-referenced examination, marking of each question would tend to be a holistic judgement that the skill upon which the question focused was either adequately displayed or not. GCE Ordinary-level competence in the present largely norm-based system would translate not to an average 35 per cent competence, whatever that may be, but to a required pattern, say something like a third-year level of competence in two specified skills and a fifth-year level in the other two. That would then be the only way of demonstrating competence: it would not be possible to compensate for a lack of third year competence in speaking by gaining a fifth year competence in reading and writing. That is what is intended by a hurdle. In the past GCE boards have tended to move away from the use of hurdles as a source of unreliability and, it was felt, potential injustice.[2] Given that the average GCE extended question is intended to discriminate throughout the range, they were justified in this view. Such hurdles demand questions focused on particular competences: the establishment of sufficiency is a different exercise from the rating of more or less.

JUDGEMENTS UNDERLYING NORMS IN STANDARDS:
LIMEN-REFERENCED ASSESSMENT

There is at least one other model of subject competence which is not discussed by Meskanskas (1976). It is the model which characterizes British public examinations. There is a clearly enunciated achievement domain. There are cutting scores though these are always modified on the basis of a scrutiny of candidates' responses rather than fixed in advance by the subject matter. The grades have at least the force of custom and the chief examiners can identify borderline grade performaces in each year's examination paper with some accuracy. The grades do not, however, carry with them any explicit definition of the achievements they imply. We shall dub it a limen-referenced model to emphasize its role in dealing with fuzzy signals implying an interdependence of transmitter and receiver.

The analysis of English Literature decisions in Appendix A, even though based on an experiment which was not designed to elucidate differences among syllabus criteria, provides strong evidence that not only are the four

1 It is worth noting in passing that, although public examinations are based on the latent-trait model, they get the worst of all worlds since the public expectation of the papers is that their difficulty should be manifest. As a result the examiners have to accept low level, and hence patchy, performances when psychometric theory indicates that precisely the opposite strategy should obtain. Little wonder that the internal consistency of such examinations is low.
2 It is impossible to generalize accurately in the GCE sector about hurdles or indeed about many other aspects of the mechanics of the grading procedure because each board has developed its own ethos. (See Forrest and Griffin (1980) for accounts of how GCE boards award grades in Advanced-level Chemistry).

boards involved invoking different criteria at different grade levels but that they are not even acting in terms of a common grading model. One board is clearly using continuum-referenced assessment while another is perhaps using a version of state-referenced assessment. Thus, by implication limen-referenced assessment as the grading approach of GCE examinations must be superordinate to both the continuum- and state-referenced models. But limen-referenced assessment has not yet been taken beyond the level of a loose framework of customary practice to the status of a descriptive model, far less a working or prescriptive model. For that development to begin there are two requirements. One may soon be met. The statement of intent[1] to make explicit the implicit subject criteria associated with each grade at 16 + will at least help to clarify at the subject level the kind of domain-referencing which is in operation. The other requirement is for some mathematical model which can be used to explore the relationship of multiple achievement criteria, no matter how implicit or explicit, to grade boundaries.

Now, if it is supposed that any achievement calls for effort on the part of the candidate and that most if not all subject examinations call for several different kinds or areas of achievement, the candidate, albeit unwittingly, will derive different degrees of satisfaction in the shape of the grade award according to how he distributes his effort across the various potential achievements. Furthermore, the pay-off from additional effort may depend on the amount of effort already expended. Such is certainly the case at the supra-subject level. Candidates at 16 + do not as a rule distribute their efforts evenly over all subjects, and where the backlog of achievement to be made up is too heavy will drop one subject to safeguard the others. Reminded that time is money, the candidate would be in no doubt that he was engaged in economic activity. The second requirement, then, the need for a mathematical model, may find its answer in the theory of economic behaviour, especially that part of the theory which is concerned with the problem of expressing choices between multi-faceted decisions on a single scale of preferences. One fruitful approach to that problem in economics is the concept of marginal utilities.

The candidate's behaviour in preparing for a whole set of subject examinations can be described as governed by marginal utilities of a rational sort.[2] But at the level of the individual subject, such rational behaviour on the candidate's part is not made easy by the relative absence

1   The recommendation (see footnote to page 4) that, in the common system of examining at 16+, grades should be clearly defined is a large step towards a more overt model of grading.

2   Significantly Blaug (1968, p. 332) notes that Bernoulli, whose theorem is fundamental to modern attempts to measure marginal utility, argues that people are guided not by the 'mathematical expectation' but by the 'moral expectation' of success. Of that, public examination boards will need little persuading!

of the two kinds of information we have suggested are requirements for a rational description of grades. To know where to put his additional effort, a decision he will make in terms of its marginal utility, the candidate must know not only the kinds of areas of achievement which influence the award of grades but also the relationship between an increase in a kind or area of achievement and an increase in the grade pay-off. That relationship is linear only in continuum-referenced assessment. In state-referenced assessment it changes with the current level of achievement.

The relationship of the three criteria elucidated by the English Literature scrutineers to the grade awards by different boards offers a ready illustration of these considerations (see Fig. 3 in Appendix A). Fig. 1 formalizes the grading model in the Oxford and Cambridge Ordinary-level English Literature examination. Unit increase in competence in any of the three criteria leads to a constant increase in grade. Fig. 2 shows the

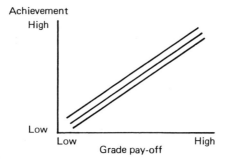

Fig. 1 Formal diagram of the relationship of achievement to grade in a norm- or continuum-referenced examination

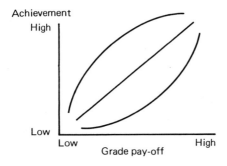

Fig. 2 Formal diagram of the possible relationship of achievement to grade: the definition of states

relationship of the same criteria to grades in the Northern Ireland Ordinary-level English Literature examination. From Fig. 3 (Appendix A) it may be seen that the 'expression of a personal response' appears (subject to the constraints on interpretation set out in Appendix A) to follow the topmost curve: there is a much greater improvement in this competence between the E/U borderline and the C/D borderline than there is between the C/D and A/B borderlines. For the candidate effort expended in this direction has increasingly marginal utility. If the starting point is low, unit increase in achievement has almost no effect on the grade pay-off. But, if a significant amount of achievement has already been realized, a further unit increase in achievement brings an enormous improvement in the grade awarded. The pay-off to the candidate increases as the amount of effort already expended increases.

On the other hand, increases in 'relevant use of knowledge' appear to enjoy a constant relation to increases in the grade award (the central relationship in the figure). Finally 'knowledge of set books' appears to conform to the bottom curve in Fig. 2. From Appendix A it may be seen that there is a relatively much smaller difference in this attribute between the E/U and C/D borderline than between the C/D and the A/B borderline. It has decreasing marginal utility for the candidate, being associated with massive early gains but reducing returns for further effort.

The major feature of Fig. 2 is that, although it is based on the judgements more or less familiar to examiners in a norm-based system, it gives rise to quite recognizable candidate 'states'. To the extent that Fig. 2 is a reasonable reflection of the basis of grade awards in English Literature by the Northern Ireland board, it would suggest that an explicit definition of grade criteria in that examination might read as follows. At the E/U borderline there is little knowledge of set books, what knowledge there is is not used relevantly and any expression of a personal response hardly gives the impression that the set books are familiar books. At the C/D borderline there is a little more knowledge used to much greater effect but the answer still has too many unsupported statements of personal response. At the A/B borderline there is a wealth of detailed knowledge, well deployed, leaving little time for more than a personal postscript to the generally acceptable response. Thus the derivation of curves of marginal utility from the borderline decisions of examiners provides a descriptive mathematical model which can encompass both continuum- and at least an approximation to state-referenced grading practice. Can it be taken one stage further to become a working model of limen-referenced assessment? Apparently a variety of practicable mathematical procedures for transforming the traditional equal interval scores or marks of a norm-based system into unequal interval scales conforming to pre-specified curves of the type described as giving rise to 'states' has been available for some time. French

(1980) quotes Fishburn (1967) and Krantz *et al.* (1971, Chapter 9) as alternatives to his own preferred technique.

In none of these techniques do the examiners need to concern themselves with marking to fit a new model. They proceed in their customary fashion: their marks are then transformed to honour their criterial weighting for each grade. Of course, as the criterial curves can be fixed long in advance of the examination, such curves would inevitably influence the examiners' decisions regarding what was in fact examined and especially the mark allocations to different aspects of the candidates' responses. (In particular these curves would provide an alternative to the all-or-nothing 'hurdles' which examiners sometimes wish to invoke but which GCE boards have tended to feel can lead to considerable injustice at the borderlines because compensation arrangements become extremely complicated.) Nevertheless, the actual transformations would be a routine computerized procedure determined by the chief examiner's desired outcome and requiring no disruption of the well-established patterns of behaviour of assistant examiners. French (op. cit., p. 17) notes that in the field of decision analysis, the

prescriptive modelling of preferences and beliefs has helped many decision makers to what they believe to be better, more consistent choices than they might otherwise have made. Moreover, it is important to note that the measurement procedures have been used by—if they will forgive me—quite innumerate decision makers. (Obviously the analyst aiding the decision maker must be competent mathematically.)

The technology is available. It is the identification of criteria that has lagged behind. It could be that, were the notion of marginal utility to be communicated to standard setters, more criteria would be forthcoming once they were comfortable that a criterion could be taken to be salient at only one, or a few, borderlines rather than having to apply throughout the range. Even those areas of experience where unsuccessful attempts carry no penalties and the emergence of rewardable behaviour is sufficient in itself can be accommodated by this limen-referenced assessment model. Grading for such subjects would be based on a large set of criteria, each of strongly increasing marginal utility. Grades would have relatively low aggregate cut-off points, and as a result just one or two accomplishments from the variety available would carry the day. A grading structure of this kind might meet the needs of such curricular innovations as the Humanities Project (Rudduck, 1976) in which the syllabus materials are intended to have value through the expansion of young minds, it being rather difficult to anticipate what shape the expansion will take.

Subjects have their own peculiar structures, *vide* the widely accepted distinction between disciplines and fields of knowledge, and these are reflected in examination syllabuses and in the examinations themselves. Mark schemes on the other hand typically ignore this diversity of structures and invoke a single model, that of an underlying latent trait as in Fig. 1. The limen-referenced approach to grading, which of course includes the latent trait model as a special case, can in principle accommodate the mark scheme to any subject structure while retaining the convenience of a single grade scale. It has all the strengths of the sampling theory of bonds (p. 50 above) in that it does not preclude a ranking of individuals along some one dimension while recognizing that the subjects of the school curriculum impose a habitual structure on the mind, although the organization of that structure is by no means always the same. It goes beyond Messick's question (p. 52 above) of the nature of the construct in recognizing that the construct, 'Physics' for example, is different at different stages in its acquisition, and that a grading scheme can as readily reflect such qualitative as it does quantitative changes in competence. All that is required of chief examiners to bring this about is that they identify explicit components of subject achievement and decide what is their value relative to each other at each grade borderline.

A STRATEGY FOR IDENTIFYING GRADE CRITERIA

A major stumbling block in the realization of limen-referenced assessment as a working model for grade definition is likely to be the initial identification of the criterial attributes of borderline performances. Art is only foremost amongst those subjects in which it is much easier to point to a grade 1 performance than it is to list the defining attributes of such a performance. Although the candidate is often required to show the development of the final product by submitting all interim productions there is still a very real problem for the candidate of knowing when a final product has been arrived at and for the examiner of knowing what kind of final product to expect. It is very difficult for the candidate in the same art folio to show a mastery of a variety of different media and styles and to show that he has developed a personal motif or stylistic identity: many candidates will achieve one or the other but not both. Must one group be regarded as superior to the other when they have simply met different criteria? (This sort of question was of concern to the HSC Investigators in 1937 (Secondary School Examinations Council, 1939, p. 18)). Any subject or aspect of subject mastery in which there is a loosely defined conglomerate of appropriate activities, which will in the long run allow of the emergence of criterial behaviours, which will be rewarded if exhibited but not necessarily penalized if absent from any particular performance, presents a problem of grade definition. Mark schemes tend to be exiguous and examiners are standardized by the simple procedure of exposing them to a series of examplars of mark or grade ranges. Clearly any procedure which can make explicit the criteria by which such subjects are graded will have general utility in identifying subject-specific grading criteria.

Hadfield (1980) has tried one possible approach to identification in the context of a CSE Art examination where the requirement is an exhibition of work and examination is by the independent ratings of visiting assessors. Part of this study concerns six assessors each of whom rated three different exhibits, one of CSE grade 1 quality, another of CSE grade 2–3 quality and a third of CSE grade 4–5 quality (that is, there were 18 exhibits in all). Each assessor was provided with 60 statements which could apply to any exhibit and was asked to sort these into 7 piles, ranging from those most characteristic of the exhibit in pile 1 to those most uncharacteristic in pile 7, with irrelevant and inapplicable statements in pile 4.

The particular strength of this Q-sort technique is that it does not involve any latent trait assumptions. Each separate statement is being judged on a present/absent dichotomy as in the state-referenced model and the status of any one attribute has only very marginal implications for the status of the other 59 statements. It is close in ethos to Thomson's bond theory, especially its notion of richness which has its counterpart in the psychology of aesthetics in the notion of 'multi-leveledness' (Kreitler and Kreitler, 1968).

The first finding of importance when each exhibit had been thus characterized was that the correlation between characterizations of good and poor exhibits averaged out to zero. There was no continuum of the latent trait type such as might be found in mathematics. In art bad is not the opposite of good; bad is different from good. A state model appears to be in operation.

Each statement was then subjected to an analysis of variance and the linear and quadratic components of its regression on exhibit quality computed. Where only the linear component is significant the straight line relationship of Fig. 2 is indicated. Thirteen statements fitted this model of which the most typical on the basis of a factor analysis were:

3   Sensitive understanding of line qualities
4   Evidence of expertise with a pencil
9   Evidence of understanding of tones.

Six statements had both the linear and the quadratic components making a significant contribution. This yields a J-shaped curve of the type associated in Fig. 2 with changing marginal utility. Typical examples were:

16   Very good grasp of one medium
36   Visually stimulating display arrangement
56   Intellectually stimulating.

All six statements had increasing marginal utility and tended, if anything, to be slightly more characteristic of middle than of high quality exhibits. One statement:

15   Evidence of individual expression,

had a significant quadratic component without any linear trend. It characterized middle grade work and was not seen as characteristic of high or low grade work. It suggests that in the Wiseman versus Cox controversy (Pilliner, 1969) about the value of multiple marking Cox may have been right at least as far as art is concerned. Cox claimed that, in averaging the marks of several raters, extreme responses were reduced to the humdrum.

Table 7   Frames of reference for grade awards and their characteristics

Criterion to which assessment is referenced	Frame of reference		Assumed model of achievement
	Performance relative to		
	(a) Other candi-dates	(b) specified syllabus material	
1. Norm	Yes	No	Linearly related to single trait
2. Domain	No	Yes	—
(a) Continuum	No	Yes	Progressive mastery of homogeneous material (discipline)
(b) State	No	Yes	Discontinuous mastery of heterogeneous material (field of knowledge)
3. Limen	—	Yes	Reflects subject structure
(a) As in current GCE practice	Yes	Yes	Reflects chief examiner's value system
(b) As might be, dependent upon the development of a working model	No	Yes	Coincides with teachers' beliefs about subject structure

Certainly in this art examination it appears that to show evidence of individuality is a high risk occupation. If the nature of one's departure from the accepted norm is as likely to offend as to delight one will receive extreme grades from different raters which when aggregated place the idiosyncratic as the quintessentially average!

In sum, Hadfield's results suggest that in the examination in question there were many routes out of the lowest grades but many fewer into the

Scaling of elements	Aggregation of elements	Major problems in interpretation of standard		
		Discontinuity in		
		(a) candidate population	(b) syllabus specification	(c) recognition of construct by new chief examiner
Linear	Unweighted sum	Yes	No	Yes
—	—	No	Yes	No
Linear	Weighted sum	No	Yes	No
Step function	Incomplete (profiles)	No	Yes	No
Potentially non-linear	Weighted sum	—	—	—
Unknown, assumed linear	Weighted sum	Yes	Yes	No
Potentially non-linear	Weighted sum	No	No	Yes

highest grades which appeared to be reserved for technically accomplished academic exercises with a pencil. This conclusion might or might not infuriate the chief examiners responsible for the grading. The point is that the Q-sort technique provides a simple procedure for feeding back to chief examiners their own operational grade definitions as a means of giving shape to a debate about what the criteria governing grades ought to be.

Once grades carry that kind of normative implication, reflecting the characteristic structures and concerns of the subject in question, limen-referenced assessment as practised in the public examinations of achievement in this country should represent a recognized, consistent and theory-grounded strategy: grade boundaries will tend to coincide with thresholds and a grade will say something fairly explicit about subject competence.

CONCLUSION

Table 7 is an attempt to summarize the characteristics of the various frames of reference for grade awards that we have surveyed in this section. It may be seen that norm-referenced assessment suits an ability rather than an achievement model although its very independence of specified syllabus material renders it potent in ensuring comparability of grade reward in different subjects taken by the same candidate population. Each year's candidate population on the other hand is a new one, so norm-referenced assessment is impotent in relation to standards over time. The restructuring of examinations and their associated grading schemes along domain-referenced lines could only result in instruments much better suited to the maintainance of standards over time. Equilibrium, however, would be sacrificed. It is unlikely that subject standards would even look interchangeable, as some subjects at least might have longer or shorter grade scales than the majority and all subjects would be at pains to emphasize the particular meanings to be attached to their grade awards.

The limen approach to grading, which we have identified with current GCE practice, is concerned to maintain equilibrium among the competing claims of a variety of possible comparabilities but in doing so lays itself wide open to both kinds of major difficulty in maintaining standards. The contest model of the implementation of standards is clearly to be seen in Criterion 3(a) of Table 7, where both the performance of other candidates and the performance relative to the specified syllabus material are cited as the frame of reference of current practice. Future development might mitigate these problems but could equally well run into others. In limen-referenced assessment, as it may develop, the major consideration in grading subject achievement will be an explicit but nevertheless subjective interpretation of how mastery of the subject develops, since only then can an ordering of various patterns of achievement be made. We do not really know much about the development of achievement. Moreover, in subjects where the various criterial components of the grade specification are dimensions rather than conglomerates of particular achievements, the freedom won in limen-referenced assessment from disruption due to syllabus specification is gained at the expense of potential misinterpretation of these relatively abstract dimensions by succeeding examiners[1]. In short, limen-referenced assessment as envisaged would doubtless be found to have its own problems but would certainly represent an improvement on limen-referenced assessment as presently practised by the examining boards.

The burden of this section is that the statistical logic of each frame of reference for grades is somewhat less than compelling. Technical reasons do not constrain the choice of grading practice. This does not mean that there is nothing to choose between them. Although neither approach is the more 'correct' in terms of its goodness of fit to what we know about educational achievement, the two approaches do vary in utility in relation to the different purposes of public examination systems. There is no real consensus as to what these purposes should be but at least an initial debate is urgently required.

1   A clear example is quoted from Houston (1980) in Appendix A, p. 89.

7 The purposes of public examination systems

Chapter 2 stressed the repeated emphasis in the inter-war years on the need for an equilibrium between the two major requirements of the public examination system, that it satisfy the needs of selectors, especially but not only in the universities, and that it say something meaningful about the educational experiences of the pupil in so far as these relate to the published syllabus. The recent Schools Council Forum on Comparability (Schools Council, 1979) develops this tradition. A dichotomy is made between comparability between subjects (which is selection oriented) and all other forms of comparability which are more or less concerned with the grade value accruing to the candidate's syllabus mastery. Chapters 4 and 5 above suggest that the notion of a dichotomy is closer to the conduct of grading meetings than any notion of equilibrium, save that which obtains in a tug of war. That war, as we have shown in Chapter 6, will not be won by technological superiority. Where might is equal, right may carry the day.

Lindquist and Hieronymus provide a succinct analysis of the diversity of purposes which examination grades might serve: 'an educational testing program has value only to the extent that the results contribute to the improvement of classroom teaching, to more effective supervisory practices, and to the better educational guidance of the pupil' (1964, p. 231). All three criteria seem equally applicable to the work of a public examination system. In this section the potential efficiency of each grading approach in furthering these ends is examined.

SELECTION

The historical function of the GCE examination system was university selection and the grading schemes were designed specifically to meet this need, witness the late inclusion of a narrow grade C at Advanced level to accommodate borderline candidates for university places. As a purpose-built system subject to the same fluctuations in supply and demand as the subject departments it serves, a truly norm-referenced grading scheme would have obvious utility for the selector. Any fragility in the assumption that the candidate does represent a commensurate unit in education does not impinge on the process of university selection. Selectors are almost always in the position of filling places not with ideal applicants but with the best of the applicants that are available. As long as selection was the dominant function of public examinations, there was no reason for the public examination system to depart from the SSEC suggested norms or from the cumulative percentile curve to which the norms applied and every reason to maintain some semblance of parity between subjects. Indeed the Robbins Committee (Committee on Higher Education, 1963) recommendation that the ratio of university places to 'qualified' applicants should be maintained has been honoured by successive governments with the result that university selectors have been able to work within a system in which any fluctuations in supply and demand affect both places available and 'qualified' applicants to approximately the same extent. Apple's (1978) question is indeed apposite:

What role does an educational system itself play in helping to create a credentialing process based on the possession (and non-possession) of this cultural capital, a credentialing system that provides numbers of agents roughly equivalent to the needs of the division of labour in society? (p. 386)

The role of the public examination system, in Apple's analysis, is the creation of high status knowledge. Such knowledge presents something of a dilemma. It

appears to be discrete knowledge. It has a (supposedly) identifiable content and (again supposedly) stable structure that is teachable and, what is critically important, testable. The arts and humanities have obviously been seen to be less amenable to such criteria, supposedly because of the very nature of their subject matter (op. cit., p. 381).

But by these criteria, high status knowledge is clearly accessible, and yet it should be, by definition, scarce. 'Its scarcity is inextricably linked to its instrumentality' (op. cit., p. 379).

Of the grading approaches we have considered only norm-referenced assessment is capable of rendering simple attainments inaccessible. It provides a simple method of stratifying individuals according to 'academic criteria', providing that the construct of academic competence remains the same (see Table 7). As long as norm-referenced assessment has this prestigious role it will be difficult to persuade any subject to move to a grading model less suited to the selection function.

There is now, however, the possibility of change. In large part, the structure of 18 + examinations, both here and abroad, is a historical legacy of an earlier need to ration scarce resources. That legacy is becoming less and less relevant to present needs. The UCCA's press advertisement issued on 5th and 7th September 1976 (UCCA, 1977, p. 15) lists only ten areas in which there were more apparently suitable candidates than places. These were Medicine, Dentistry, Pharmacy, Veterinary Science, Accountancy, Law, Architecture, Psychology, Drama and Fine Art. An equivalent number of subject areas were noted as having as many apparently suitable candidates as places while the remainder (and the majority) including Engineering (except Civil), Technology (all courses), Foreign Languages, Economics, Mathematics, Physics and Chemistry all had more places than apparently suitable candidates. Thus in many university departments selection as a problem has almost disappeared and what is required is qualification, the assurance that particular skills have been acquired.

The nature of the qualification as instanced by the pattern of experience implied—that is, the domain to which the qualification is referred—is becoming a problem particularly in science departments which increasingly have to resort to additional first year courses to even out the discrepancies in content between one Advanced-level syllabus and another, albeit of the same name. This divergence in qualification between selected candidates is further exacerbated by the GCE tradition of distinguishing very precisely between an examination and a teaching syllabus.

Most examination syllabuses allow of a multiplicity of teaching syllabuses through the practice of allowing a choice of questions, a practice not easily incorporated in a state-referenced system. Thus, although a move to a domain-referenced grading system with a more closely specified achievement domain would not greatly inconvenience university selectors and might well facilitate the transition from school to university science department, such a move might be seen in the schools as an unwelcome reassertion of university dominance of the sixth form curriculum were the choice of strategy within syllabuses to be severely curtailed.

The university influence on the later years of schooling is now much weakened with the upward trend in the school leaving age and the increasing democratization of post-compulsory education, but the selection-oriented approach is difficult to slough off. No meaning has ever officially attached to GCE grades and so the only meaning they have is a conventional one. To change the convention in such circumstances may be felt to invite chaos, but chaos is not a foregone conclusion. A change away from any suggestion of a norm-referenced system would be a change from a conventional to a meaningful grading system which need not be impotent with regard to selection.

The chief examiners and their subject panels have already taken on the task of defining Advanced levels of approximately uniform demand by reference to their best judgement. Were they also to be allowed to identify cut-off scores indicative of meaningful degrees of proficiency an alternative to the candidate as unit of measurement would emerge. In the context of selection an emphasis on subject-specific grading criteria would produce equally practicable though differently interpreted outcomes.

Only in one major respect are the domain-referenced approaches a less flexible response to the demands of selection. In 1946 it was decided that too high a proportion of candidates passed in HSC. Over a five-year period the pass rate was moved in all subjects by an average 5 per cent of candidates. (Petch, 1953, p. 159). Persuading examiners to change the criterion of an acceptable performance would be a less easy manoeuvre and persuading them to stay in line almost impossible.

It follows that for purposes of selection the norm-referenced approach is by far the more flexible, through its open invitation to add, divide and reify grades which nevertheless can be readily adjusted to refer to whatever is convenient at the time.

EDUCATIONAL GUIDANCE OF THE PUPIL

This aspect of grading procedure in public examinations is rarely given the status of an important purpose. The results of public examinations come at the end of long periods of instruction, too late, it is felt, to have any impact on how the student responds to that instruction. To the extent that they are summative evaluations, the only guidance to the pupil is vocationally oriented. The student who wishes to know whether his career chances are better in mathematics or history is told: You have/have not some insight into the nature of history; you have/have not some insight into the nature of mathematics. Now decide what you want to be. If you are interested in the state of the competition, the GCE statistics will tell you how many others have reached your level of competence in each field.

Such a view, however, ignores the extent to which the pupils' behaviour may be shaped by the requirements of the examination. This aspect of 'backwash' seems to await systematic investigation: evidence is purely anecdotal. One might suppose, however, that it is relatively unusual for school candidates to have seen the actual syllabus statement issued by a GCE board and customary for them to have at least some and often an intimate acquaintance with previous examination questions.

Becker and his colleagues (1961, 1968) have observed American freshmen students over a sufficient period of time to provide detailed evidence of the stratagems employed and the cues used by students to cope with their intense concern about their academic performance. So pervasive is this concern with evidence on which to base self-evaluation that it has been elevated into a comprehensive theory of achievement motivation. (Veroff, 1969).

How may the sixth-form student fare in his search for self-evaluation given the following fairly typical circumstances? In a norm-referenced system, many of the examination questions which represent acquaintance with the demands of the subject will have been expressly designed to allow for a considerable range in adequacy of response. Unless his teacher is also an examiner for the examining board, the teacher will have little idea of the board's marking practice which tends not to be seen by any of the boards as requiring wide dissemination[1] and hence will have little option but to resort to some fairly direct ranking of the pupils in his charge. The pupil for his part may then, knowing how his immediate predecessors fared under the same teacher, translate his position among his peers into an expectation of passing. Should the expectation turn out to be one of failing, there would be plenty of time for that expectation to shape his behaviour: teachers are not the only potential agents of self-fulfilling prophecies. If there were to be a change of teacher, rendering prediction more problematic, uncertainty would be increased and might lead to debilitating levels of anxiety.

Perhaps the most relevant analysis of the mechanism of the self-fulfilling prophecy is due to Weiner's (1974 and 1979) attribution theory. Students who enjoy a fair measure of successful coping early in a school course tend to attribute their success to ability and see themselves as more able. This leads them to expect a continued high rate of success. Failure is unexpected and attributed to lack of effort or bad luck. This attribution leads to some shame and increased effort after failure. On the other hand students who perceive their attainments as low see themselves as low in ability and therefore expect failure. Success is unexpected and attributed to good luck which does not affect future expectancies which continue to be low. In fact, children who perceive their attainment as high are more task-oriented in the classroom than those who perceive their attainment as low (Nicholls, 1976).

Inequality of effort and its increase with age appears an inevitable outcome of a classroom in which assessment is based on relative competence. The higher motivation of high achievers appears dependent on the presence of lower achievers for whom the presence of high achievers leads to lack of motivation. Segregating high and low achievers is no solution. David (1966) and Werts and Watley (1969) report evidence which suggests that average students at selective American colleges may give up graduate school aspirations even though they may be superior to top students at mediocre colleges who had their graduate school aspirations strengthened by a level of performance high only in relation to the mediocre performance of their peers.

An alternative strategy is to attempt to induce more equality of effort by directing the student's attention, not to his peers, but to the task in hand. Ames *et al.* (1977) have shown that non-competitive learning arrangements appear to offer possibilities of fostering attributions for success and failure and the pleasure concomitant upon these attributions that will lead to

1   The JMB has recently changed its policy in this regard and plans to produce 'a new kind of publication . . . in which specimens of candidates' answers are discussed by the examiners' (Joint Matriculation Board, 1979).

effort in low as well as high achievers. Their prescription conforms closely to the principles of mastery learning (Block, 1971) which is supported by and indeed depends upon domain-referenced assessment procedures. Were the emphasis in public examinations to shift towards an attainment standard with a consequent tighter syllabus specification and more salience attached to meeting particular criteria, the behaviour of teacher and pupils could be expected to become more task-oriented. Whether the anticipated changes in motivation and eventually in learning would also ensue remains a matter for future research.

It may well be felt that there are too many imponderables in the argument for it to carry much weight and that consideration of the public examination system should be confined to the summative role. On the other hand, if some formative influence is allowed, one must at least accede to Bloom's (1968) limited conclusion that the evaluative procedures that lead to the most effective feedback to students are often not those that lead to the tidiest ranking of students. And it would be as well to note at least the title of Maehr's (1976) paper, 'Continuing motivation: an analysis of a seldom considered educational outcome'.

IMPROVEMENT OF CLASSROOM TEACHING

The teacher in his classroom deals with only a tiny and seldom representative sample of the candidate population in his subject. For the teacher, then, there will be no difference between the feedback from a continuum-referenced examination and from a norm-referenced examination. Both will be able to show some impact of his pedagogical initiatives and both will provide the information too late to shape his behaviour with the current group. A move to state-referenced assessment and eventually perhaps a profile report might be more informative but might equally well be seen as an infringement of the teacher's autonomy.

Examination arrangements can only be used to improve instruction if teachers are prepared to accept the examining boards as appropriate sources of curricular authority. The evidence suggests that at present the yoke of the examination boards sits lightly upon them. Gillham (1977) has documented the failure of the 'Special Syllabus' option offered almost since their inception by the university examining boards and continued by the GCE boards and, while he does not exonerate the boards, he considers it likely that conservative teacher attitudes have constituted a considerable barrier to innovation.[1]

1 In 1928 Crofts and Jones noted that 'every Examining Body makes provision for the consideration of special syllabuses submitted by a school or group of schools; if approved, special question papers are set on these syllabuses at a charge which by no means covers the cost of setting, printing, and moderating. Very few special syllabuses are now submitted. Some years ago the Joint Matriculation Board offered to make no charge for such special papers, but even then the number did not show an appreciable increase' (pp. 39–40).

The public examination system has had its procedures sanctified by long usage and teachers have been cautious in their attitudes to changes in it even where these increase their professional autonomy (p. 60).

Reid and his colleagues at Birmingham (Schools Council, 1976), investigating the shaping influence of the GCE Advanced-level examinations on sixth form curricula, found the same conservative acceptance of the familiar, although Christie and Griffin (1973) found 66 % of teachers prepared to accept the public examination boards as curriculum development agencies at 16 +. Nevertheless, the response to syllabuses as at present formulated may be a poor guide to the response to a much more highly detailed domain specification.

Such a specification would almost certainly be seen as university inspired. Shipman (1971) observes that the universities through their Ordinary- and Advanced-level requirements act to support a concentration in the schools on a narrow range of subjects and on formal teaching within these. He discerns in the Working Papers of the Schools Council and the syllabuses of the public examination boards

two different and diverging worlds of education. One is firmly planted in revered academic traditions, is adapted to teaching from a pool of factual knowledge and has clearly defined, if often irrelevant, subject boundaries. The other is experimental, looking to America rather than our own past for inspiration, focuses on contemporary problems, groups subjects together and rejects formal teaching methods . . . The projects in O and A level courses in Mathematics, Sciences and Languages financed by the Nuffield Foundation have produced teaching material for traditional subjects after considering the key elements in each discipline. The parallel developments in the Humanities under the Schools Council have started instead by considering relevance as a basis for choosing new content, materials and teaching methods, regardless of the usual subject categories (p. 104).

Shipman reminds us that there is more than one kind of instruction to improve. Clearly defined packets of factual knowledge tied to the key elements of a discipline are the very essence of subject domains. A move to specify further these domains, especially if allied to a shift to continuum-referenced grading would, we suggest, reinforce the divergence and, with the authority of the universities behind it, render the Humanities position almost untenable. But we would suggest that Shipman has under-emphasized the more insidious, probably inadvertent, influence of the universities on the secondary school curriculum. The implied damage arises from the insistence that, for ease of selection, all subjects should be graded in the same way. Only the full development of the limen-referenced grading system in which the structure of the domain is allowed to determine the structure and value of the marking scheme—the curriculum coming first, so to speak—could accommodate both of Shipman's worlds and yet result in a single grade system common to all subjects. Good might be done by stealth!

The further brake on the improvement of instruction adumbrated by Shipman is the tendency for a highly articulated domain statement to emphasize content and for that content to assume an undue importance which renders it inviolable. Burnet (reported in McPherson and Neave, 1976), writing in 1917 of the effect of external written examinations on the classical curriculum, said that the written examination can only deal successfully with that part of it which is destined to be forgotten as soon as it has served its purpose and it can tell us next to nothing of what is to remain as a possession for ever. This has always been a hard criticism for any syllabus to answer but a champion is now to hand.

Broudy (1977) offers the thought that

in addition to the more familiar modes of knowing—knowing *how* and knowing *that*—there is also and perhaps always an implicit knowing *with* . . . knowing *with* furnishes a context within which a particular situation is perceived, interpreted and judged. Contexts can function without being at the centre of consciousness, without being recalled verbatim, and without serving as hypothetical deductive premises for action. (p. 12).

Almost all public examinations seek to measure content before it becomes context. The domain-referenced examination system in offering a more detailed and more categorical definition of what content deserves to become context might, with luck, provide a syllabus which irked if for no other reason than that it was hard to avoid. Such a syllabus we might anticipate would be subjected to the most minute and searching scrutiny. Therein lies the best hope for the improvement of instruction.

THE SUPERVISORY FUNCTION

It is in terms of the supervisory function ('public accountability' is the current phrase) that the relative utilities of the three frames of reference summarized in Table 7 most obviously differ. Norm-referenced grading systems can react only marginally to changes over time in the achievements of the individuals making up the entry. Yet, is it not the very purpose of education to engender such changes? Little wonder then that, in England and the U.S.A., the public examination system has manifestly failed the educational decision-maker at the national level.

Standardized (i.e. norm-referenced) achievement testing is a multi-million dollar industry in the United States. Yet it has been deemed worthwhile to commit a few millions more to National Assessment. 'National Assessment is . . . concerned with . . . identifying the things that defined groups of students can do. The model of standardized testing is NOT the model of National Assessment. (In standardized testing it is not essential to know what high achievers *know* or what average achievers *know* but only that some assessees know more than others' (Womer, 1970, p. 7). National Assessment is an attempt to monitor in the United States what Becker (1964) has called 'human capital', the developed productive capabilities of citizens.

In Britain secondary schools may now spend more on examination fees than their entire 'capitation grant', i.e. recurrent expenditure on text books, paper, chalk and all other classroom consumables (Montgomery, 1978, p. 9). Yet the impact on national achievement of the most sweeping post-war educational decision, the abolition of selective secondary schools in the public sector, remains unassessed, although there is a continuing, and confused, debate with reference to public examination results.[1] In a norm-referenced examination system, it is still possible to use the results to establish the value added by different sectors of the educational system, but only if the different sectors are competing for the same awards (Christie and Griffin, 1970). The efficiency of the system as a whole cannot be directly evaluated. National standards may rise or fall without affecting grade awards which are arrived at simply by ranking the performances of candidates. System changes may change standards without affecting the relative performance of different candidate groups. The confusion created sufficient governmental concern for the setting up of a national pro-gramme, under the aegis of the Department of Education and Science, to monitor educational standards[2]. How then can the public examination boards defend their share of the education budget?

PUBLIC EXAMINATIONS AND PUBLIC ACCOUNTABILITY

The efficiency of educational systems is a matter of prime concern to those who are interested in education's contribution to the development of society. If the systems are to be improved, procedures must be developed for evaluating them. We must 'specify definite performance levels for pupils as they move through and out of the schools, so that we can gauge how the educational system is doing in its attempts to help them deal with the occupational, social, cultural and moral demands of the world they are to enter' (Dyer, 1967, p. 18).

That evaluation could be made were the public examination boards allowed to adopt a truly domain-referenced grading policy. 'The criterion-referenced approach is probably making its greatest contribution in the monitoring, and assessment of instructional strategies and outcomes' (Hieronymus, 1972, p. 63). The statement, 'I got all my sums right', is domain-referenced. The meaningfulness of the statement is not dependent

1 See, for example, Baldwin (1979) and ensuing correspondence in the Times Educational Supplement.
2 Assessment of Performance Unit (1977).

on comparison with other testees. Nevertheless, one can ask 'How many other children got them all right?' and get the same information as a norm-referenced assessment would give. But one might equally well ask: 'What kind of sums were they?', an irrelevant question in a norm-referenced approach. The question asked of domain-referenced grades depends upon the social values one wishes to emphasize in the education system. Domain-referenced grading does not banish the notion of success and failure, but success and failure are now so defined that the success of one candidate does not prejudice the success of another. It becomes genuinely possible that all shall pass, and as in the Caucus-race, everyone shall have prizes. It is the equal possibility that all shall fail and no one have prizes which makes it so much more potent a source of information on which to base educational decision making.

A move to domain-referenced grading would allow of the monitoring of national standards by public examination boards. There would be no immediate need for massive examinations development if the initial change were no more than a shift to a limen-referenced grading scheme in which candidate norms were ignored (bottom line of Table 7). The change would involve little more than that a quantification of the subjective interpretation of the marks of the chief examiner should become not merely the salient, but the sole criterion, for grade awards. The chief examiner would have to be able to interpret examination marks in terms of specified levels of competence but in the short-term development of the limen model the only specification that is required for these levels of competence is that the levels of attainments currently associated with each Advanced-level grade should be maintained in the future. There is no change of role for the chief examiner. As now, he must judge whether the difficulty of the questions or the calibre of the candidates has changed from the year of inception of the system. As now, he must make his judgement without knowledge of the effect of his decision on the proportions of candidates in each grade.

The only new requirement is an agreement with and among GCE boards, the DES and the Schools Council on a clear order of priorities for the 'standards' that are to be maintained. The chief examiners must be free to make final grading decisions in terms of the standards of attainment of previous years without reference to expectations imported from other subjects or to probabilities of success that obtained in the past.

In such a process the technical sophistication of board secretaries would not be squandered. Boards would indeed depend in the final analysis on an intuitive act but, with a clear directive to maintain standards of attainment over time, the energies of the boards' secretaries would be directed to bolstering the confidence with which that step could be taken. The move towards the incorporation of objective test components in most examinations can only facilitate this endeavour by bringing the technology of item banking to bear (Schools Council, 1971). As indicated in Chapter 5, some of the statistical assumptions required of such ingenious units as Choppin's WITS (Choppin, 1976) may be too highly constraining to allow of statistical direction from that source in many subjects. But in that minority of subjects well suited to continuum-referenced grade definition, a major step forward in grading accuracy could be made. State-referenced subjects would derive benefit from the other dimension of item banking—more formal approaches to item-writing (e.g. Bormuth, 1970; Hively, 1974). Even though these by no means eliminate subjectivity (Roid and Haladyna, 1978), they do offer the possibility of a more closely controlled definition of the achievement domain in terms which are immediately utilizable by the examining team. There is already a general tendency for examination syllabuses to be markedly longer, largely because they now spell out the syllabus requirements in much more detail. Further developments in the direction of precise specification encouraged by the above trends would eventually lead in state-referenced subjects to quite precise guidance from the generalizability model (Cronbach *et al.*, 1972), a statistical approach which is as applicable to essay questions as to objective items. Its major constraining assumption is that the degree of interrelatedness of the achievements sampled from a domain should be constant within a domain. The weakness or strength of the relationship is irrelevant as is the number of domains which are identified as relevant. Effectively one is not tied to a single trait or a multi-trait model of achievement.

Developments such as these could provide cogent statistical back-up rather than the present potent statistical challenge. Moreover, no commensurate increase in technical sophistication is required of users of the certificates. In the early stages the published grades would be 'the recipe as before' and any changes would be gradual, as far as possible affecting only the availability of candidates with specified grades, not the competence associated—now overtly—with these grades. American experience with the C.E.E.B. Scholastic Aptitude Test indicates that there would be little difficulty in adjusting to any eventual divergence in grade proportions between different subjects.

The Scholastic Aptitude Test (SAT) measures verbal and mathematical aptitudes, separately reported (Angoff, 1971). As an aptitude test, it is in the norm-referenced tradition but the norm is the performance of the entry in 1956. Thus it can be deemed to be continuum-referenced in the sense that every candidate's result is reported relative to that fixed yardstick (though no meaning is adduced to that yardstick). SAT results are currently causing a furore in the U.S. since they reveal a marked drop in the verbal aptitude of candidates over the last two decades. That kind of feedback about the performance of the educational system, only adumbrated in the Christie and Forrest (1980) study as a result of considerable additional effort and expense, has been made routinely available through a deliberate decision to build the grading schemes upon comparability of standards over time.

Any measurements of an educational system should reflect the changes that occur in that system with the passage of time. Society looks to the results of public examinations for an estimate of the progress of the system. Yet the proposed common system of examining at 16 + will proceed on the assumption that subject-specific grade criteria would be nice rather than that they are necessary. The exigencies of selection are still in conflict with performance feedback to the educational system.

However, the difficulties of a full-blooded domain-referenced approach should not be underestimated. Over a span of years changes within a subject can range from a wholesale revision of the syllabus content to a subtle reorientation of the stated objectives. As the Christie and Forrest (1980) pilot experiment has shown, as soon as the differences in syllabuses and the associated examinations become great special problems arise in the maintenance of achievement standards and it would probably be necessary in the transition years to use comparability of grade proportions, i.e. opportunity. For example, when the Schools Council's N and F proposals were being actively considered it was proposed to make the grading transition from GCE Advanced level, not so much by being specifically norm-referenced, but rather by providing a normative basis for the development of subject-specific grade criteria. But this is no more than to maintain the *status quo* in which no one is clear as to the precise frame of reference of grading schemes and certainly offers no guarantee that the development of the eventual frame of reference will be uniform at the level of boards, of syllabus development committees or even of chief examiners. In our view a more fundamental commitment is required. We have suggested a partial redress of the current difficulties faced by GCE boards through a primary emphasis on stability of attainment over time in the grading system. A deliberate espousal of this grading emphasis might well lead in the long term to criterion-referenced examinations, 'deliberately constructed to yield measurements that are directly interpretable in terms of specified performance standards' (Glaser and Nitko, 1971, p. 653).

SOME CONCLUSIONS AND A RECOMMENDATION

The burden of the preceding discussion is that public examination grading arrangements have several purposes and might well vary to accommodate different purposes. The publication of examination results is a fundamental educational practice particularly in need of empirical investigation with respect to the purposes and values it serves. No large scale survey of users which might illumine the debate about purposes has come to our attention and yet the question is not beyond the reach of empirical investigation. Stake (1970), in discussing the evaluation of educational programmes, urges that more attention be given to empirical studies of the grades and values that determine criteria of performance. Purposes as well as practices require examination.

This focus would solve most of the outstanding comparability problems. A means would then be available for establishing comparability of standards within subjects, and in particular for providing a means of monitoring the many thousands of Mode III alternatives which are at present available in CSE and which are likely to be carried forward into the common system of examining at 16+. It would also provide a means of establishing comparability between the subject syllabuses of the different boards. Such advances would be won at the expense of any direct attempt to maintain a putative comparability of difficulty among subjects; nevertheless if subject-specific criteria can be established and maintained over time any apparent discrepancies in subject difficulty will at least be held constant over the years and comparability, if not equivalence, of between-subject standards maintained.

This decision to abandon the aptitude interpretation of academic standards would clarify for the examining boards the entire grading problem in their examinations. More to the point, it might profit education well. It would shift attention and effort from often arid statistical exercises in establishing after the event whether comparability had been maintained to consideration of how the criteria enunciated for each subject could be best attained. More important still, the very enunciation of subject-specific criteria would lead to a continuing investigation of the relevance, appropriateness and suitability of contemporary syllabuses and examinations to the needs of pupils, schools and colleges and to the demands of the society of which they are part, that is, to the identification of meaningful achievement criteria for our education system, difficult though that task will prove to be.

References

Ames, C., Ames, R. and Felker, D. (1977). 'Effects of competitive reward structure and valence of outcomes on children's achievement attributions', *Journal of Educational Psychology*, **69**, pp. 1–8.

Anderson, R. C. (1969). 'The comparative field experiment: an illustration from high school biology', in *Proceedings of the 1968 Invitational Conference on Testing Problems*. Princeton, N. J.: Educational Testing Service.

Anderson, R. C. (1977). 'The notion of schemata and the educational enterprise: general discussion of the conference', in R. C. Anderson, R. J. Spiro and W. E. Montague (eds.) *Schooling and the Acquisition of Knowledge*. Hillsdale, New Jersey: Lawrence Erlbaum.

Angoff, W. H. (ed.) (1971). *The College Board Admissions Testing Program: a technical report on research and development activities relating to the Scholastic Aptitude Test and Achievement Test*. New York: College Entrance Examination Board.

Apple, M. W. (1978). 'Ideology and educational reform', *Comparative Education Review*, **26**, III, 367–387.

Argyle, M. (1976). 'Personality and social behaviour' in R. Harré, (ed.) *Personality*. Basil Blackwell.

Assessment of Performance Unit. See Department of Education and Science, (1977).

Atkinson, J. W. (1974). 'Motivational determinants of intellective performance and cumulative achievement' in J. W. Atkinson and J. O. Raynor (eds.) *Motivation and Achievement*, pp. 398–410. Washington, D.C.: V. H. Winston.

Baird, L. L. and Feister, W. J. (1972). *Grading standards: the Relation of Changes in Average Student Ability to the Average Grades Awarded* (RB-71-28). Princeton, New Jersey: Educational Testing Service.

Baldwin, R. W. (1979). *Performance of GCE A level in Maintained Schools*. Esher: National Council for Educational Standards.

Bardell, G. S., Forrest, G. M. and Shoesmith, D. J. (1978). *Comparability in GCE: A Review of the Board's Studies, 1964–1977*. Manchester: Joint Matriculation Board on behalf of the GCE examining boards.

Bartlett, F. C. (1932). *Remembering: a Study in Experimental and Social Psychology*. Cambridge University Press.

Becker, G. S. (1964). *Human Capital*. New York: Columbia University Press.

Becker, H. S., Geer, B., Hughes, E. C. and Strauss, A. L. (1961). *Boys in White:*

Student Culture in a Medical School. Chicago: University of Chicago Press.

Becker, H. S., Geer, B. and Hughes, E. C. (1968). *Making the Grade: the Academic Side of College Life*. New York: Wiley.

Bennett, S. N. (1978). 'Recent research on teaching: a dream, a belief and a model', *British Journal of Educational Psychology*, **48**, 2, 127–147.

Blaug, M. (1968). *Economic Theory in Retrospect*. Heinemann Educational.

Block, J. (1971). *Mastery Learning*. New York: Holt, Rinehart and Winston.

Bloom, B. S. (ed., 1956). *A Taxonomy of Educational Objectives: The Classification of Educational Goals. Handbook I: Cognitive Domain*. Longmans, Green.

Bloom, B. S. (1968). 'Learning for mastery', *Evaluation Comment*, **1**. University of Los Angeles, California.

Bloom, B. S., Hastings, J. T. and Madaus, G. F. (1971). *Handbook on Formative and Summative Evaluation of Student Learning*. New York: McGraw-Hill.

Bloomfield, B., Dobby, J. and Duckworth, D. (1977). *Mode Comparability in the CSE: a Study of Two Subjects in Two Examining Boards* (Schools Council Examinations Bulletin 36). Evans/Methuen Educational.

Board of Education (1914). *Examinations in Secondary Schools. Proposals of the Board of Education* (Circular 849). HMSO.

Board of Education (1938). *Secondary Education with Special Reference to Grammar Schools and Technical High Schools* (The Spens Report). HMSO.

Board of Education (1939). *Education in 1938*. HMSO.

Bormuth, J. R. (1970). *On the Theory of Achievement Test Items*. Chicago: University of Chicago Press.

Broudy, H. S. (1977). 'Types of knowledge and purposes of education' in R. C. Anderson, R. G. Spiro, and W. E. Montague, (eds.) *Schooling and the Acquisition of Knowledge*. Hillsdale, New Jersey: Erlbaum.

Bruner, J. S. (1960). *The Process of Education*. Harvard University Press.

Carroll, J. B. (1976). 'Psychometric tests as cognitive tasks: a new "structure of intellect"' in L. Resnick, (ed.) *The Nature of Intelligence*. Hillsdale, New Jersey: Erlbaum.

Choppin, B. H. (1976). 'Recent developments in item banking: a review' in D. N. M. de Gruyter, and L. J. T. van der Kamp, (eds.) *Advances in Psychological and Educational Measurement*. New York: Wiley.

Choppin, B. H. L., Orr, L., Kurle, S. D. M., Fara, P. and James, G. (1972). *The Prediction of Academic Success*. Slough: National Foundation for Educational Research.

Christie, T. and Forrest, G. M. (1980). *Standards at GCE A-level: 1963 and 1973* (Schools Council Research Study). Macmillan Education.

Christie, T. and Griffin, A. (1970). 'The examination achievements of highly selective schools', *Educational Research*, **12**, 3, 202–208.

Christie, T. and Griffin, A. (1973). *Teachers' Views on a New Administrative Structure for Secondary School Examinations*. Joint Matriculation Board.

Christie, T. and Mills, J. (1973). *The Use of a Scholastic Aptitude Test in University Selection*. Department of Education, University of Manchester (mimeo).

Committee on Higher Education (1963). *Higher Education* (The Robbins Report). HMSO.

Crofts, J. M. and Jones, D. C. (1928). *Secondary School Examination Statistics*.

Longmans, Green.

Cronbach, L. J., Gleser, G. C., Nanda, H. and Rajaratnam, N. (1972). *The Dependability of Behavioural Measurements: Theory of Generalizability for Scores and Profiles*. New York: Wiley.

Dahllöf, U. (1971). *Ability Grouping, Content Validity and Curriculum Process Analysis*. New York: Teachers College Press.

David, J. A. (1966). 'The campus as a frog pond: an application of the theory of relative deprivation to career decisions of college men', *The American Journal of Sociology*, **72**, pp. 1–16.

Department of Education and Science (1977). Assessment of Performance Unit, *An Introduction*. HMSO.

Department of Education and Science (1978a). *School Examinations* (The Waddell Report). HMSO.

Department of Education and Science (1978b). *Statistics of Education, Vol 2, 1976, School Leavers: CSE, GCE*. HMSO.

Department of Education and Science (1978c). *Curriculum 11–16: Modern Languages*. A working paper by the Modern Language Committee of HM Inspectorate.

Department of Education and Science (1979). *Statistics of Education, Vol. 2, 1977, School Leavers: CSE, GCE*. HMSO.

Duckworth, D. and Entwistle, N. J. (1974). 'Attitudes to school subjects: a repertory grid technique', *British Journal of Educational Psychology*, **44**, pp. 76–82.

Dyer, H. S. (1967). 'The discovery and development of educational goals' in *Proceedings of the 1966 Invitational Conference on Testing Problems*, pp. 12–24. Princeton, New Jersey: Educational Testing Service.

Ebel, R. L. (1962). 'Content standard test scores', *Educational and Psychological Measurement*, **22**, pp. 11–17.

Emrick, J. A. (1971). 'An evaluation model for mastery testing', *Journal of Educational Measurement*. **8**, pp. 321–326.

Estes, W. K. (1974). 'Learning theory and intelligence', *American Psychologist*, **22**, pp. 740–747.

Fairbrother, R. W. (1975). 'The reliability of teacher's judgements of the abilities being tested by multiple choice items', *Educational Research*, **17**, 3, 202–210.

Fishburn, P. C. (1967). 'Methods for estimating additive utilities', *Management Science*, **13**, pp. 435–453.

Forrest, G. M. (1971). *Standards in Subjects at the Ordinary Level of the GCE, June, 1970* (Occasional Publication 33). Joint Matriculation Board.

Forrest, G. M. and Griffin, A. (1980). *Report of the Inter-board Cross-moderation Study in GCE Chemistry (Advanced), 1978*. Joint Matriculation Board.

Forrest, G. M. and Smith, G. A. (1972). *Standards in Subjects at the Ordinary Level of the GCE, June 1971* (Occasional Publication 34). Joint Matriculation Board.

French, S. (1980). *Measurement Theory and Examinations* (Notes in Decision Theory, Note No. 88). Department of Decision Theory, University of Manchester.

Gagné, R. M. (1962). 'The acquisition of knowledge', *Psychology Review*, **69**, pp. 355–365.

Gillham, B. A. (1977). 'The reluctant beneficiaries: the teacher and the public examination system', *British Journal of Educational Studies*, **XXV**, Pt. 1, 50–62.

Glaser, R. (1963), 'Instructional technology and the measurement of learning outcomes', *American Psychologist*, **18**, pp. 519–521.

Glaser, R. and Nitko, A. J. (1971). 'Measurement in learning and instruction' in R. L. Thorndike, (ed.) *Educational Measurement*, pp. 625–670. 2nd ed. Washington D.C.: American Council on Education.

Goldstein, H. (1979). 'Consequences of using the Rasch Model for educational assessment', *British Educational Research Journal*, **5**, 2, 211–220.

Government Observations on the Tenth Report of the House of Commons Expenditure Committee. Session 1976–77 'The Attainments of the School Leaver' (1978). (Cmmd. 7124) HMSO.

Hadfield, G. (1980). 'Sources of variation in what constitutes "good" art examinations at age sixteen plus' (unpublished M.Ed. dissertation). University of Manchester.

Hambleton, R. K., Swaminathan, H., Algina, J. and Coulson, D. B. (1978). 'Criterion-referenced testing and measurement: a review of technical issues and developments', *Review of Educational Research*, **48**, 1, 1–148.

Hecker, P. C. and Wood, R. (1979). *Report of a Cross-moderation study in Physics at Advanced level: 1977*. University of London, University Entrance and School Examinations Council.

Hieronymus, A. N. (1972). 'Today's testing: what do we know how to do?', in *Proceedings of the 1971 Invitational Conference on Testing Problems*. pp. 57–68. Princeton, New Jersey: Educational Testing Service.

Hively, W. (1974). 'Introduction to domain-referenced testing', *Educational Technology*, **14**, pp. 5–10.

House of Commons Expenditure Committee (1977). *The Attainments of the School Leaver* (Tenth Report). HMSO.

Houston, J. G. (1980). *Report of the Inter-board Cross-moderation study in English Literature at Ordinary level: 1975*. The Associated Examining Board.

Hunt, E. (1971). 'What kind of computer is man?', *Cognitive Psychology*, **2**, pp. 57–98.

Husén, T. (1974). *The Learning Society*. Methuen.

Inglis, W. F. J. (1980). 'A content analysis of 'O' and 'A' level papers on modern British and European History set by two GCE examination boards', *British Educational Research Journal*, **6**, 1, 43–52.

Joint Matriculation Board (1973). *Seventieth Annual Report*. Joint Matriculation Board.

Joint Matriculation Board (1975). *Seventy-second Annual Report*. Joint Matriculation Board.

Joint Matriculation Board (1979). *Seventy-sixth Annual Report*. Joint Matriculation Board.

Kelly, A. (1976). 'A study of the comparability of external examinations in different subjects', *Research in Education*, **16**, pp. 37–63.

Krantz, D. H., Luce, R. D., Suppes, P. and Tversky, A. (1971). *Foundations of Measurement Vol. 1*. New York: Academic Press.

Kreitler, M. and Kreitler, S. (1968). *Psychology of the Arts*. Durham, North

Carolina: Duke University Press.

Lennon, R. T. (1972). 'Theory and technology of norming' in C. H. Bracht *et al.* (eds.) *Perspectives in Educational and Psychological Measurement.* Englewood Cliffs, New Jersey: Prentice-Hall.

Lindquist, E. F. and Hieronymus, A. N. (1964). *Manual for Administrators, Supervisors and Counselors: Iowa Tests of Basic Skills.* Boston: Houghton Mifflin.

Macintosh, H. G. (1969). 'The place of tests in secondary education (entrance, attainment and terminal) and their use in selecting for higher education' in K. Ingenkamp, (ed.) *Developments in Educational Testing, Vol. 2.* University of London Press.

Marklund, S. (1969). 'The predictive value of school marks and tests for higher education in Sweden' in J. A. Lauwerys and D. G. Scanlon (eds.) *Examinations: the World Year Book of Education 1969.* Evans.

McIntyre, D. and Brown, S. (1978). 'The conceptualisation of attainment', *British Educational Research Journal*, **4**, 2, 41–50.

McPherson, A. F. and Neave, G. (1976). 'Innovation and the organisation of educational knowledge', *Higher Education Review*, **8**, Pt. 3, 41–52.

McVey, P. J. (1978). 'Are public examinations fair to science students?', *Physics Education*, **13**, I, 28–32.

Maehr, M. L. (1976). 'Continuing motivation: an analysis of a seldom considered educational outcome', *Review of Educational Research*, **46**, 31, 443–462.

Magnusson, D. and Endler, N. S. (eds.) (1977). *Personality at the Crossroads: Current Issues in Interactional Psychology.* Hillsdale, New Jersey: Lawrence Erlbaum.

Mather, D. R., France, N. and Save, G. T. (1965). *The Certificate of Secondary Education: A Handbook for Moderators.* Collins.

Meskanskas, T. A. (1976). 'Evaluation models for criterion-referenced testing: views regarding mastery and standard setting', *Review of Educational Research*, **46**, Pt. I, 133–158.

Messick, S. (1975). 'The standard problem: meaning and values in measurement and evaluation', *American Psychologist*, **30**, pp. 955–966.

Miles, H. B. (1973). *Some Correlates of Academic Performance of Pupils in Secondary Schools.* Social Science Research Council Project, HR 469.

Millman, J. (1973). 'Passing scores and test lengths for domain-referenced measures', *Review of Educational Research*, **43**, 21, pp. 205–216.

Ministry of Education (1948a). *Education in 1947.* HMSO.

Ministry of Education (1948b). 'Standards' in the examination for the General Certificate of Education (Letter from the Ministry of Education, dated 23 June 1948).

Ministry of Education (1951). *Education 1900–1950.* HMSO.

Ministry of Education (1960). *Examinations in Secondary Schools: The General Certificate of Education* (Third Report of the Secondary School Examinations Council). HMSO.

Montgomery, R. (1978). *A New Examination of Examinations.* Routledge.

Musgrove, F. (1971). *Patterns of Power and Authority in English Education.* Methuen.

Nedelsky, L. (1954). 'Absolute grading standards for objective tests', *Educational and Psychological Measurement*, **14**, pp. 3–19.

Newbould, C. A. and Massey, A. J. (1979). *Comparability Using a Common Element* (Occasional Publication 7). Cambridge: Test Development and Research Unit.

Nicholls, J. G. (1976). 'When a scale measures more than its name denotes: the case of the Test Anxiety Scale for children', *Journal of Consulting and Clinical Psychology*, **44**, pp. 976–985.

Novick, M. R. and Jackson, P. H. (1974). *Statistical Methods for Educational and Psychological Research*. New York: McGraw-Hill.

Nuttall, D. L. (1971). *The 1968 CSE Monitoring Experiment* (Schools Council Working Paper 34). Evans/Methuen Educational.

Nuttall, D. L. (1973). *Mode Comparability: Comparability of Standards as between Modes of Examining in The West Yorkshire and Lindsey Regional Examining Board*. The West Yorkshire and Lindsey Regional Examining Board.

Nuttall, D. L. and Willmott, A. S. (1972). *British Examinations: Techniques of Analysis*. Windsor: National Foundation for Educational Research.

Nuttall, D. l., Backhouse, J. K. and Willmott, A. S. (1974). *Comparability of Standards Between Subjects* (Schools Council Examinations Bulletin 29). Evans/Methuen Educational.

Ormerod, M. B. and Duckworth, D. (1975). *Pupils' Attitudes to Science: a Review of Research*. Slough: National Foundation for Educational Research.

Pask, G. (1976). 'Styles and strategies of learning', *British Journal of Educational Psychology*, **46**, pp. 128–148.

Petch, J. A. (1953). *Fifty years of Examining: the Joint Matriculation Board 1903–1953*. Harrap.

Peterson, A. D. C. (1975). 'The 16–19 age group: curriculum and examinations in Europe', *International Review of Education*, **21**, pp. 165–176.

Piaget, J. (1971). *Biology and Knowledge: An Essay on the Relations Between Organic Regulations and Cognitive Processes*. Chicago: University of Chicago Press.

Pilliner, A. E. G. (1969). 'Multiple Marking: Wiseman or Cox? Research Note', *British Journal of Educational Psychology*, **39**, pp. 313–5.

Popham, W. J. (1974). 'An approaching peril: cloud referenced tests', *Phi Delta Kappan*, **56**, pp. 614–615.

Popham, W. J. (1975). *Educational Evaluation*. Englewood Cliffs, New Jersey: Prentice-Hall.

Popham, W. J. and Husek, T. R. (1969). 'Implications of criterion-referenced measurement', *Journal of Educational Measurement*, **6**, pp. 1–9.

Rasch, G. (1960). *Probabilistic Models for some Intelligence and Attainment Tests*. Copenhagen: Danmarks Paedagogiske Institut.

Reid, G. H. and Haladyna, T. M. (1978). 'A comparison of objective-based and modified-Bormuth item writing techniques', *Educational and Psychological Measurement*, **38**, pp. 19–28.

Rudduck, J. (1976). *Dissemination of Innovation: the Humanities Curriculum Project* (Schools Council Working Paper 56). Evans/Methuen Educational.

Schools Council (1966). *The 1965 CSE Monitoring Experiment* (Schools Council Working Paper 6, Pts. I and II). HMSO.

Schools Council (1971). *Question Banks: Their Use in School Examinations*

(Schools Council Examinations Bulletin 22). Evans/Methuen Educational.

Schools Council and Standing Conference on University Entrance (1973). *Preparation for Degree Courses* (Schools Council Working Paper 47). Evans/ Methuen Educational.

Schools Council (1975a). *Examinations at 16 + : Proposals for the Future.* Evans/Methuen Educational.

Schools Council (1975b). *The Whole Curriculum 13–16* (Working Paper 53). Evans/Methuen Educational.

Schools Council (1976). *Sixth Form Syllabuses and Examinations: a New Look* (Schools Council Research Study). Macmillan Education.

Schools Council Forum on Comparability (1979). *Standards in Public Examinations: Problems and Possibilities* (Comparability in Examinations, Occasional Paper 1). Schools Council.

Scott, J. F. (1975). *Comparability of Grade Standards in Mathematics at GCE A level* (Schools Council Examinations Bulletin 30). Evans/Methuen Educational.

Schroder, H. M., Driver, M. J. and Streufert, S. (1967). *Human Information Processing.* New York: Holt, Rinehart and Winston.

Secondary School Examinations Council (1927). *Reports of the Investigators appointed to inquire into the methods and standards of awards in the eight approved Second Examinations held at Midsummer, 1926.* Secondary School Examinations Council.

Secondary School Examinations Council (1939). *The Higher School Certificate Examination: being the Report of the panel of investigators appointed by the Secondary School Examinations Council to enquire into the eight approved Higher School Certificate examinations held in the summer of 1937.* HMSO.

Secondary School Examinations Council (1947). *Examinations in Secondary Schools.* HMSO.

Secondary School Examinations Council (1960). *The General Certificate of Education and Sixth Form Studies* (Third Report). HMSO.

Secondary School Examinations Council (1963). *The Certificate of Secondary Education: Some Suggestions for Teachers and Examiners* (Examinations Bulletin No. 1) HMSO.

Secondary School Examinations Council (1964). *The Certificate of Secondary Education: an introduction to some techniques of examining* (Examinations Bulletin No. 3). HMSO.

Seddon, G. M. (1978). 'The properties of Bloom's Taxonomy of Educational Objectives for the cognitive domain', *Review of Educational Research,* **48**, 2, 303–323.

Shipman, M. D. (1971). 'Curriculum for inequality?' in R. Hooper (ed.) *The Curriculum: context, design and development.* Edinburgh: Oliver and Boyd.

Shoesmith, D. J. and Massey, A. J. (1977). *Grading Standards in Mathematics at Ordinary level in 1976: a Cross-Moderation Study.* Cambridge: Test Development and Research Unit.

Shoesmith, D. J., Newbould, C. A. and Harrison, A. W. (1977). *A common element in GCE French examinations.* Oxford and Cambridge Schools Examination Board (on behalf of the GCE Examining Boards).

Spearman, C. (1927). *The Abilities of Man.* Macmillan.

Spielberger, C. D. (ed., (1972)). *Anxiety: Current Trends in Theory and Research, vols. I and II.* New York: Academic Press.

Stake, R. E. (1970). 'Objectives, priorities, and other judgement data', *Review of Educational Research*, **40**, pp. 181–212.

Sumner, R. (ed., (1977)). *Monitoring National Standards of Attainment in Schools.* Windsor: National Foundation for Educational Research.

Thomson, G. H. (1939). *The Factorial Analysis of Human Ability.* University of London Press.

Thorndike, E. L. (1905). 'The quantitative study of education', *Forum*, **36**, pp. 443–8.

Thorndike, E. L., Bregman, E. O., Cobb, M. V. and Woodyard, E. (1926). *The Measurement of Intelligence.* New York: Teachers College Columbia U.

Universities Central Council on Admissions (1977). *Fourteenth Report, 1975–76.* The Universities Central Council on Admissions.

University of London Entrance and School Examinations Council (1972). *Advanced level Physics Comparability Study.* University of London.

Veroff, J. (1969). 'Social comparison and the development of achievement motivation' in C. P. Smith (ed.) *Achievement-related Motives in Children.* New York: Russell Sage Foundation.

Wankowski, J. A. (1969). *GCE's and Degrees* (Research report—mimeo). University of Birmingham.

Weiner, B. (1974). *Achievement Motivation and Attribution Theory.* Morristown, New Jersey: General Learning Press.

Weiner, B. (1979). 'A theory of motivation for some classroom experiences', *Journal of Education Psychology*, **71**, 1, 3–25.

Weir, A. D. (1975). 'The Scottish Certificate of Education: factors affecting pupil performance', *Scottish Educational Studies*, **7**. Pt. I, 5–14.

Welsh Joint Education Committee (1973). *Standards in Subjects at GCE Ordinary level, June 1972* (Research report No. 4). Welsh Joint Education Committee.

Werts, C. E. and Watley, D. J. (1969). 'A student's dilemma: Big fish–little pond or little fish–big pond', *Journal of Counseling Psychology*, **16**, pp. 14–19.

Willmott, A. S. (1977). *CSE and GCE Grading Standards: the 1973 Comparability Study* (Schools Council Research Study). Macmillan Education.

Willmott, A. S. and Fowles, D. E. (1974). *The Objective Interpretation of Test Performance: The Rasch Model Applied.* Slough: National Foundation for Educational Research.

Winter, D. G. and McClelland, D. C. (1978). 'Thematic analysis: an empirically derived measure of the effects of liberal arts education', *Journal of Educational Psychology*, **70**, Pt. I, 8–16.

Womer, F. B. (1970). *What is National Assessment?.* Denver, Colorado: National Assessment of Educational Progress.

Wood, R. (1976a). 'A critical note on Harvey's "Some thoughts on norm-referenced and criterion-referenced measures" ', *Research in Education*, **15**, pp. 69–72.

Wood, R. (1976b). 'Trait measurement and item banks' in D. N. M. De Gruijter and L. J. Th. van der Kamp (eds.) *Advances in Psychological and Educational Measurement.* John Wiley.

Appendix A
Evidence for differences in the bias of demands between GCE boards

In common with the examiners in the Physics study, Houston (1980) reports that his English Literature scrutineers 'remarked not only upon the difficulty of identifying the norms and of relating these to the work of candidates for the different boards' examinations, but stressed the even greater difficulty of identifying the agreed criteria, especially the one that related to a response to literature. Several felt that their judgements had been confounded by the clearly different approaches of the various boards.' (p. 14). However, thanks to the full account of the results in Tables 3, 4 and 5 of the report and the well conceived experimental design, it is possible to quantify these uncertainties as they apply to the norms, the criteria and the boards and to use these estimates as indices of error against which to evaluate the significance of the findings (Table A1).

The design of the study is as follows. Five senior examiners from GCE boards not involved in the scrutiny were asked to evaluate the scripts of 120 candidates, 10 at each of the A/B, C/D and E/U borderlines from the remaining four GCE boards. They were not required to apply their own standards. Rather they had to read the forty scripts at any borderline and allow these forty scripts to provide the 'norm' referred to above. That average performance was graded as 3 on a five-point scale, the same scale being used at all three grade borderlines, though of course the meaning of 3 differs according to the norm set at each borderline (a dramatic example of the lack of relationship between a norm-referenced scale and any notion of an absolute standard). What was to be evaluated was agreed by the scrutineers on the basis of a separate representative sample of 10 scripts, 2 from each grade for each board. Only criteria acceptable to all scrutineers were to be used in the study and they settled on three of these:

  (i) knowledge of set books,
  (ii) relevant use of knowledge,
 (iii) expression of a personal response. (p.6)

The 120 scripts were individually assessed on the five-point scale for each criterion in turn.

The omission of the voluminous data on individual candidates from the published report is only to be expected. It does not affect our analysis since we choose to define all differences between raters as random error. The norm-based assessment is so designed that there should be no differences overall between the criteria, the grade levels, the raters or their interactions. The only unconstrained source of variation is the boards themselves. Should one board be demanding significantly more of a criterial attribute than the others at a particular borderline, its 10 borderline candidates will evidence more of that attribute and tend to be graded 5, well above average relative to the norm set by all 40 candidates at that borderline. (Clearly the norm is based as much on the work of this board as of any other so that there is—in the design—an inherent conservative tendency to minimize differences.) Thus, while the other sources of variance should always average to 30 (3 times 10 candidates, the basic unit of analysis) the board average can vary between 50 and 10 as can any of its interactions. Table A1

Table A1   Analysis of variance in mean mark of borderline scripts due to criterion of evaluation, level of borderline GCE board and scrutineer

Source	Sums of squares	d.f.	Mean square	F	Significance
Rater(R)	677.44	4	169·44	—	
Criterion(C)	398·23	2	199·12	1·67	n.s.
R × C	956·16	8	119·52		
Grade(G)	193·43	2	96·72	2·68	n.s.
R × G	288.29	8	36·04		
C × G	46·64	4	11.66	1·14	n.s.
R × C × G	164·31	16	10·27		
Board(B)	586·46	3	195·49	7·12	$p < 0.01$
R × B	329·68	12	27·47		
C × B	24·66	6	4·11	< 1.0	n.s.
R × C × B	108·95	24	4·54		
G × B	765·59	6	127·60	9·86	$p < 0.01$
R × G × B	310·69	24	12·94		
C × G × B	87·54	12	7·30	2·25	$p < 0.05$
R × C × G × G	156·18	48	3·25		
TOTALS	5094·55	179	—		

shows the extent to which these fluctuations differ significantly from the chance expectation set by the variation in the scrutineers' reading of the scripts.

In the absence of data from individual scripts, it is not possible to evaluate the extent to which each rater kept to the required norm, but these norms have been successfully implemented collectively by the scrutineers in relation to the criteria and the grade levels (C, G, and $C \times G$ are all non-significant sources of variation). Similarly, on the basis of the collective judgement of the scrutineers, the boards did not differ from each other in the overall weight they attached to the three criteria ($C \times B$ non-significant) confirming the prior decision of the scrutineers that each criterion was equally applicable to each board.

The remaining sources are all significant. There are real differences in the overall quality of the scripts provided by each board ($F = 7.12$ with 3, 12 d.f.) but these differences cannot be interpreted since the relative severity of the four boards changes according to which borderline is under scrutiny ($F = 9.86$ with 6, 24 d.f.). Finally, we cannot even generalize at this level, since differences in relative severity at different borderlines themselves differ according to the criterion under scrutiny ($F = 2.25$ with 12, 48 d.f.). This significant $C \times G \times B$ interaction is set out in Fig. 3 which illustrates the different emphases of the various boards that militate against any easy conclusions as to the comparability of their standards.

From the point of view of grading, Oxford and Cambridge is the most straightforward case. Their borderline candidates show knowledge and use of that knowledge which closely accords with the norms set by all four boards together. At no borderline is there much evidence of personal expression. The inference is that the Oxford and Cambridge board do not make as much demand for this kind of response as do the other boards. Most notably, from the point of view of the models described in Chapter 6 of the main text, the profiles at each grade borderline in this board are identical. Only Oxford and Cambridge of the four boards illustrated is using continuum-referenced grading. The difference between grade levels is simply that each one requires more of the same. The Northern Ireland board on the other hand is using an approximation to state-referenced grading. Their E/U borderline candidates are quite strong on knowledge for that level but clearly lack the expression of a personal response which has presumably helped to depress their grade. Improvement in that respect clearly pays handsome dividends and this criterion is more clearly in evidence at the C/D borderline in the Northern Ireland board than in any other Board. The A/B borderline shows yet another shift in emphasis: while use of knowledge and personal response are again very much in evidence, knowledge of set books is clearly the distinguishing factor. Thus the criteria for grades in the Northern Ireland board vary with the grade. At each grade boundary a different pattern of response is in evidence. This is one version of a state-referenced grading system, lacking only the notion of a clear hierarchy of all-or-none performances to be a typical exemplar.

There is a suggestion of this kind of state-referencing in both the remaining boards. In the Welsh Joint Education Committee the relative salience of knowledge and the use made of that knowledge changes significantly and regularly from grade to grade, and in precisely the opposite direction from the non-significant trend in the same relationship in the Associated Examining Board. Both boards also exhibit disordinal interactions between their overall relationship to the criterial norms and the grade level (these have created the significant board-by-grade interaction). This may imply that the four boards have simply failed to maintain comparable standards at each grade level. But if one cared to assume that grade comparability had been maintained, then the implication would be that in the WJEC the knowledge of set books component

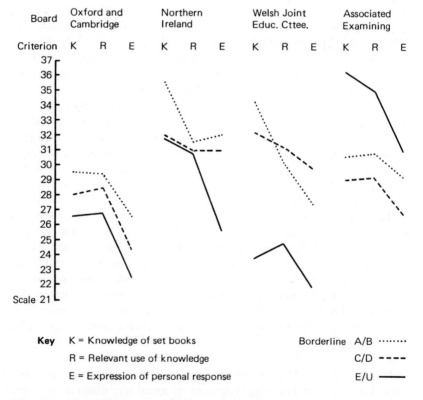

Fig. 3 The board by criterion by level interaction in English Literature Ordinary level (based on Houston, 1980)

may well be much more important than in the other boards—challenging the initial assumption of an equally weighted composite of the three criteria—and that in the AEB there may be some further very important criterion which has not been taken into account—challenging the scrutineers' initial assumption that a separate criterion dealing 'specifically with the control of language' (op. cit. p. 6) would be unnecessary. It is this reciprocal relationship between the constitution of the standard and the establishment of comparability of standards which is the very nub of the problem.

Appendix B
Evidence for the empirical differentiation of aptitude and achievement as reference criteria in GCE Physics (Advanced)

In the Advanced-level Physics Comparability Study (University of London Entrance and School Examinations Council, 1972) five separate predictors were regressed on the Physics A-level grades of nine GCE boards yielding an expected mean Physics grade in each case. The predictors represent two major criteria, aptitude and subject achievement. They were

Aptitude 1:	TAA V, a verbal multiple choice test
Aptitude 2:	TAA M, a mathematical multiple choice test
Achievement 1:	a Physics multiple choice test
Achievement 2:	a Physics essay type test
Achievement 3:	Achievement 1 + 2.

The results in Table B1 are abstracted from Table 12 of the report.

These data are subjected to an analysis of variance in Table B2 which leads to the following conclusions. The effects due to criteria (aptitude v. achievement) and tests within criteria (the five bases of prediction) are negligible. The present authors are only puzzled that there is any variance at all associated with these sources, as in the regression method indicated by

Table B1 Expected mean grades by board on the basis of five separate predictors

Board	Apt. 1	Apt. 2	Ach. 1	Ach. 2	Ach. 3
1	2·59	2·56	2·59	2·59	2·51
2	2·93	2·95	3·10	3·12	3·17
3	2·96	2·94	3·05	2·96	3·01
4	2·78	2·86	2·54	2·83	2·67
5	2·85	2·94	2·78	2·73	2·73
6	3·14	3·07	3·35	3·08	3·25
7	2·93	2·88	2·95	2·81	2·88
8	3·02	3·00	2·96	2·87	2·93
9	2·81	2·78	2·59	2·93	2·75

the report the grand expected mean should always coincide with grand observed mean and thus be the same in all five cases.

Table B2   Analysis of variance in expected mean grades by board

Source	Sums of squares	d.f.	Mean square	F
Criteria	9·633	1	9·633	
Tests within C	0·722	3	0·241	
Boards	13546·400	8	1693·300	
B ×C	1262·933	8	157·876	2·15 with 8·24df.
B ×T within C	1763·112	24	73·463	
TOTALS	16582·800	44	—	

The main effect of boards is irrelevant, merely indicating that the samples of candidates drawn from the nine boards can be expected to differ in their mean Advanced-level grades.

The focus of the analysis is the board by criterion (B × C) interaction which indicates the extent to which each board received comparable treatment under each criterion. This effect is significant at the 10 per cent level ($F = 2·36$ for $p < 0·05$). It refers to the difference between say board 2 which has a higher expected mean grade under an achievement than aptitude criterion and, say, board 8 where the position is reversed and aptitude leads to a higher expected mean grade than does achievement. The extent of such divergences in the table would occur one time in ten by chance and is thus only indicative of a potential effect rather than conclusive proof that the effect exists.

However, we have two grounds for anticipating that, were achievement to be actual Advanced-level achievement as in a cross moderation exercise, the effect would be strengthened. The monitoring achievement tests in this experiment were administered in the month before the Advanced-level examinations. Scott (1975), in a particularly elegant approach to the problem of between-board comparability, has shown not only that there is differential growth in achievement in Mathematics in the lead up to the examinations as a function of the achievement in the mock examination but that there is a considerable unpredictable element in this growth associated with the individual classroom group. In other words, achievement is not a stable attribute during the period of intensive preparation.

Secondly, while the Physics study does not report the correlations between the aptitude variables and the achievement predictors, the statement that the inclusion of the aptitude tests made 'no appreciable difference' (op. cit. p. 21) to a multiple regression analysis implies that the correlation between aptitude and the achievement-based predictors must have been rather higher than the correlation between aptitude and the achievement criterion, suggesting that the achievement-based predictors are contaminated with unwanted aptitude variance for the purposes of our comparison.

Appendix C
Data on the relation between Ordinary level and Advanced level achievement in 1963 and 1973

A-level grade	1963 Number of candidates	Average no. of O-levels Passed	Failed	Entered	1973 Number of candidates	Average no. of O-levels Passed	Failed	Entered
MATHEMATICS								
A	10	6·30	0·90	7·20	14	8·29	3·43	8·71
B	17	6·71	1·24	7·94	21	7·76	0·33	8·10
C	15	6·40	1·13	7·53	5	7·00	0·40	7·40
D	14	6·00	1·64	7·64	17	6·94	1·00	7·94
E	16	6·50	1·25	7·75	21	6·90	1·19	8·10
O	22	5·41	1·95	7·36	9	6·78	0·78	7·56
F	6	4·00	2·50	6·50	13	4·92	2·00	6·92
ENGLISH LITERATURE								
A	15	7·40	0·53	7·93	15	8·13	0·20	8·33
B	16	6·44	1·06	7·50	22	6·68	1·14	7·82
C	13	5·38	2·15	7·54	10	5·30	2·10	7·40
D	17	5·24	2·12	7·35	12	6·08	1·42	7·50
E	21	4·95	2·33	7·29	24	5·29	1·63	6·92
O	14	5·86	1·86	7·71	12	4·67	2·50	7·17
F	4	5·00	2·25	7·25	5	3·00	4·20	7·20
CHEMISTRY								
A	11	6·27	1·09	7·36	14	8·00	0·29	8·29
B	12	7·50	0·42	7·92	17	7·94	0·41	8·35
C	3	6·67	0·67	7·33	10	7·20	0·90	8·10
D	19	6·53	0·79	7·32	12	6·50	1·08	7·58
E	29	6·62	1·21	7·83	20	6·85	0·85	7·70
O	12	5·33	2·00	7·33	23	6·87	1·43	8·30
F	14	5·50	2·14	7·64	4	5·00	3·00	8·00

Index